The Pleasure in Drawing

The Pleasure in Drawing

JEAN-LUC NANCY

TRANSLATED BY PHILIP ARMSTRONG

FORDHAM UNIVERSITY PRESS ✦ *New York* 2013

This work was originally published in French as Jean-Luc Nancy, *Le Plaisir au dessin* © 2009 Éditions Galilée, Paris.

This work has been published with the assistance of the French Ministry of Culture—National Center for the book.

Ouvrage publié avec le concours du Ministère français chargé de la culture—Centre National du Livre.

Library of Congress Cataloging-in-Publication Data
Nancy, Jean-Luc.
    [Plaisir au dessin. English]
    The pleasure in drawing / Jean-Luc Nancy ; translated by Philip Armstrong.
        pages cm
    Summary: "Originally written for an exhibition Jean-Luc Nancy curated at the Museum of Fine Arts in Lyon in 2007, this book addresses the medium of drawing in light of the question of form—of form in its formation, as a formative force, as a birth to form. In this sense, drawing opens less toward its achievement, intention, and accomplishment than toward a finality without end and the infinite renewal of ends, toward lines of sense marked by tracings, suspensions, and permanent interruptions"—Provided by publisher.
    Translation of: Plaisir au dessin.—Paris : Hazan ; Lyon : Musée des beaux-arts de Lyon, c2007.—239 p. : ill. (some col.) ; 28 cm.
    Includes bibliographical references.
    ISBN 978-0-8232-5093-6 (hardback)—ISBN 978-0-8232-5094-3 (paper)
    1. Drawing—Philosophy.   I. Armstrong, Philip, 1962- translator.
II. Title.
NC17.F7L96713   2013
741.01'17—dc23

                                                    2013014020

19 18 17 16   5 4 3 2
First edition

Contents

Translator's Note

The Pleasure in Drawing is a translation of *Le Plaisir au dessin*, a text by Jean-Luc Nancy first published in French in 2007. The initial version of the text was published as the opening essay to the catalogue accompanying an exhibition on drawing that Nancy had been invited to curate with Sylvie Ramond and Eric Pagliano for the Musée des Beaux-Arts in Lyon.[1] Under the same title but with a number of significant modifications, the text was reprinted in 2009 as a book published by Éditions Galilée, part of the "Écritures/Figures" series, edited by Michel Delorme. (The Galilée version includes a number of illustrations that were not included in the original catalogue or exhibition.[2]) The translation is based on the version published by Galilée.

The text is composed of sixteen separately titled sections. Between each section of the text, Nancy has placed a *Carnet de croquis*, a "Sketchbook" of quotations from different writers, artists, or philosophers on art. He notes that these "sketchbooks" can be read in the order in which they appear or leafed through independently of the text. In the original, the quotations include the titles of books or essays from which they have been taken, but there are no footnotes provided for any of the quotations. The text itself also includes several quotations that have no source or footnote. As Nancy states in a note appended to the beginning of the text: "it is not necessary here to become burdened by erudition." Translating the text has thus posed a number of problems, notably when Nancy cites English texts in translation or texts in French or from other languages in which English translations already exist. Whenever possible, I have tried to use these existing translations, even when no source or footnote is given in either the original or this translation. However, there are a few occasions where the existing translation for a quotation has not been found. And there are a number of occasions when existing translations have been modified in order to follow the emphasis Nancy places on certain terms.

Translating the title of Nancy's text has proved no less challenging, notably in light of Nancy's insistence throughout his writings on the role that prepositions play in our thinking, in other words, in rethinking and rearticulating the relation between thought and the object *of* thought, as well as our relation *to* and *with* one another. The expression *le plaisir au dessin* is already unusual in French, since the more common expression and accompanying preposition would be *le plaisir de*, as in the pleasure one takes in doing something. A similar idiom with the preposition *à* exists, but usually this is a contraction of the pleasure one takes or one finds in doing something. At the same time, *au dessin* in the title evokes expressions like *au travail* ("at work") or *à l'œuvre* (as in the phrase *à l'œuvre on connaît l'artisan*, "you can tell an artist by his work"). I hope that, translated as *The Pleasure in Drawing*, the title at least evokes the pleasure that might be taken in the act of drawing, the pleasure that draws, as well as the pleasure that exists in drawings, not as a theme but as a force or design. In this sense, certainly, another possibility for the title could be *Drawing Pleasure*.³

The reference to *dessin* or "drawing" throughout the text also relates to Nancy's references to *dessein*, usually translated as design, as in the design of an object or a project design, but which also refers to an intention—*à dessein* is to do something deliberately, by design, on purpose. When Nancy brings the two terms together by referring to *dess(e)in* (one of the section titles is *Le dess[e]in des arts*), thus evoking the frequent substitution between drawing and design that existed in texts up until the eighteenth century, I have found no other option for translating *dess(e)in* than "drawing/design." However, it should also be recalled that *dess(e)in* suggests close proximity to the German *Dasein*, the familiar term for "existence" that Heidegger uses for "being" or "being there," whose implications Nancy exploits throughout the text. Perhaps more tendentiously, *dess(e)in* suggests some proximity to *des seins*, which Nancy has explored further in his text "La naissance des seins" (translated into English as "The Birth of Breasts")—again, this question of birth and its relation to (finite) being will appear with some frequency in the text that follows, one of the conditions for thinking the pleasure in drawing.⁴

Finally, a word concerning Nancy's frequent use of reflexive verbs in the text. While it is common to translate reflexive verbs into the passive form in English, the use of phrases such as *se demande lui-même*—where the additional "itself" or *soi-même* supplements the existing reflexive verb—offers a different set of challenges. Rather than translating this as "its self" each time—as in something that "makes demands on its self"—we have referred more simply to "itself." However, we should recall that the terms of this reflexivity refer less to an interiority, self-enclosure, or self-identity than a condition in which the self—the "itself"—is defined by its "own" exteriority to its "self," and hence (in Nancy's terms) *exposed*. The self exposes itself to (or toward) its self ("From Self Toward Self" is one of the section titles), opening a gap or displacement within any self-reflexivity. This use of the reflexive verb form recurs with some frequency in the pages that follow.

For their help in the translation, or for finding sources for quotations, I would especially like to thank Matthieu Branlat, Claire Farago, Lisa Florman, Laura Lisbon, Stephen Melville, and Ginette Michaud. Jennifer Branlat reviewed every word with a wonderfully scrupulous and careful eye—needless to say, any remaining errors are my own. Helen Tartar offered just the right advice and extraordinarily generous help in bringing the translation to completion. As ever, Jean-Luc Nancy was perfectly gracious in answering questions and suggesting solutions.

Preface to the English-Language Edition

Drawing: this word in English suggests drawing out, stretching, and extracting. One can *draw* a line and *draw* a lesson. In French, one can draw out [*tirer*] a line or a lesson, but it is impossible to draw [*dessiner*] a lesson. Or rather, *dessiner* a lesson in French means something entirely different from "drawing" it. It would be to give an illustration, a visual representation of its contents, as when Plato asks his reader to draw a line in the mind that he will then divide into proportional segments in order to better understand the relation between the sensible and intelligible.

In French, *dessiner* a lesson is to make it be seen, to show and present it to an intuitive grasp. *Tirer* a lesson is to gather the lessons learned from a specific event that itself is not a lesson: for example—and again from Plato—to conclude from Socrates' moral qualities that physical ugliness can harbor a wealth of ideas.

To show, to conclude, ostension, inference: gestures that, indeed, come together by way of one or another fine point, whether it is the point of a stylus, a finger, or a mind. However, that does not mean that these terms and their translation into different languages end up by overlapping one another. On the contrary—it is well known that there is never any homothety between languages, and precisely this lack gives to the task of translation its pleasurable and disturbing character. When I read *drawing* in English, knowing that I ought to be thinking of *dessin*, I feel myself carried far away on a sea of complexity, all the while knowing that there will be something to discover, an island of sense, or even just a current or turbulent zone.

This is also why one experiences so much gratitude to whoever holds the rudder of this perilous navigation—in this case, the sturdy hands of Philip Armstrong. (At the edge of the ocean, Helen Tartar sets out beacons and markers for landing.)

*   *   *

Between drawing out and showing—an asymptotic contact—there is something to discover. To show, to make something seen, to designate—*designare*—is also what accompanies the de-monstration through which a conclusion or lesson is drawn. One draws—one traces or extracts—in order to show. One shows by extending or spreading out in front of oneself. Better, in order to show something well, in order to render it fully manifest, one must not cease drawing (if only to draw attention), and in order to draw out (trace or pull), one must not lose sight of the invisible extremity of the mark [*trait*], the point by which the line advances and loses itself beyond itself in its own desire.

The gesture of showing by extending—extending in order to show or bring to light, extracting the lineament and incision of a form, contour, sense, or idea from the shadow or a compact mass—such is the gesture of *existing*. A sketch (*Entwurf*), Heidegger says, a term for which one retains above all the meaning of *jet* (*werfen*—"throwing, casting"), of projection toward what continues to come [*le non-advenu*], leaving in shadow the value of the mark, the tracing out, the form in the process of forming itself.

To exist is to sketch oneself [*s'esquisser*]. One would like to write *s'exquisser*—to open oneself to a form which shows itself in the movement of its uprising [*surgissement*]. No one would consent to live if they did not experience this desire—to open oneself to the desire of (letting oneself) being drawn to the outside.

J-L.N.
August 2012

The Pleasure in Drawing

Form

Drawing is the opening of form. This can be thought in two ways: opening in the sense of a beginning, departure, origin, dispatch, impetus, or sketching out, and opening in the sense of an availability or inherent capacity. According to the first sense, drawing evokes more the gesture of drawing than the traced figure. According to the second, it indicates the figure's essential incompleteness, a non-closure or non-totalizing of form. In one way or another, the word *drawing* retains a dynamic, energetic, and incipient value that does not exist in words like *painting*, *film*, or *cinema*. By contrast, words like *music*, *dance*, and *poetry*, or words like *speech* and *song*, come closer to preserving a dynamic or potential within any actual or static value. *Drawing* participates in a semantic field where act and force [*puissance*] are combined, or where the sense of the act, the state, or the being that is in question cannot be detached entirely from a sense of gesture, movement, or becoming. The word *drawing* draws itself along or draws itself forward before all disposed form, all tracing out [*tracé*], as if initiating a trace that must always be discovered again—opened up, opened out, initiated, incised.[1]

In the idea of *drawing*, the word itself can also designate an essential suspension of an achieved reality. "Here is a drawing by Rembrandt" only gives us the impoverished factual and informational meaning of the word, whereas the expression "Rembrandt's drawing" reveals a quite different value. For *Rembrandt's drawing* is Rembrandt's own manner of drawing. It is the collection of characteristics that distinguish his drawing. Furthermore, it is also the role that drawing plays in his work, the way drawing plays itself out within the work, either within the paintings or as a separate exercise, whether in sketches, studies, or engravings. "Rembrandt's drawing" tends to distinguish itself only from "Rembrandt's color," an expression that designates the proper manner according to which Rembrandt employs color or colors (their hues, nuances, relationships, etc.). (For the moment, we will leave aside the very delicate and undoubtedly inextricable sharing—division, exchange, and combination—between color and drawing).

As a propensity, then, "Rembrandt's drawing/color" is "Rembrandt" himself, or "Rembrandt's art." This singularity or originality is situated beyond style or talent. Irreducible to any form of analysis, it is no doubt best indicated by affirming this singularity or originality as "art," in other words, as a *savoir-faire* or know-how that exceeds all knowledge and all making. This is not a question of "genius" (a word about which we should remain guarded, and for good reason), but rather the thought of this excess, a thought of the unthinkable and unfeasible (the unspeakable and the unrealizable). Each time that it takes place, this thought as such can only be *single* and *singular*, without possible substitution, like all truth.

In the idea of *drawing*, there is the singularity of the opening—the formation, impetus, or gesture—of form, which is to say, exactly what must not have already been given in a form in order to form itself.[2] Drawing is not a given, available, formed form. On the contrary, it is the gift, invention, uprising [*surgissement*], or birth of form. "That a form comes" is drawing's formula, and this formula implies at the same time the desire for and the anticipation of form, a way of being exposed to what comes, to an unexpected occurrence, or to a surprise that no prior formality will have been able to precede or preform.

Sketchbook 1

"Think of Cézanne's drawing, which, in a word, aims at what comes into appearance [*l'apparaître*] beneath appearance"

—Yves Bonnefoy, *Remarks on the Gaze*

"Composition is the drawing (up) of the work, but the work's drawing is the work itself. The work is drawn (up). Drawing is thus not a secondary art: preliminary or remnant of another art. No more is it an art among others. It is an art quite a-part, and what there is of art in all art."

—Éliane Escoubas, "'The Happy Hand': Kandinsky and Composition"

"The work of drawing—that where there best arises the rapid trajectory of thought and blindness unified."

—Antonio Saura, in *Pierre Alechinsky: Excerpts on the (Por)trait*

"The omnipresent Line in its spacing from every point to every other in order to institute the Idea."

—Stéphane Mallarmé, *Music and Letters*

"A round and assured wandering of a curve that enlaces, delicate intertwining like brushwood, or construction made from angles and straights lines—no matter, drawing is always what comes first, what is assumed to spring forth from nothing."

—Jean-Christophe Bailly, *The Infinite Studio*

Idea

But what is it, then, that we call *form*? It is imperative to take up this problem, since *drawing* represents par excellence the element of form, or a form—and, as we have suggested, not only within the domain of the visual arts but in all artistic domains, since in all these domains one can discern a register, element, or valence to which the idea of drawing lays claim—without being simply a metaphoric use of the term.[3]

Leonardo da Vinci writes: "These parts [of music] are constrained to arise and to die in one or more harmonic tempos which surround a proportionality by its members; such a harmony is composed not differently from the circumferential line which generates human beauty by its [respective] members."[4]

Form is the "idea," recalling the word chosen by Plato to designate the intelligible models of the real. *Idea* signifies for Plato, according to the Greek term, nothing other than "visible form" (to which one might add that the "visible" is form's primary register of reference, because that register maintains form in the foreground, distinct, and in this way "formed." By contrast, and according to another distinction, *drawing* [*dessin*] opens form to its own formation). In fact, the most recent translations of Plato substitute "Form" for the more traditional "Idea." "Intelligible form" takes nothing away from the field of the visible; it demands only that this visibility adapt, not to the immediate and interested perception of things, but to the judgment and aim [*visée*] of their sense and truth. Just as the visible form of the table presents us with its use and affordance [*disponibilité*] as furniture, whether for eating, writing, or climbing up on, so the "idea" of the table (*tabula rasa*, multiplication table, tablature) carries the sense of a general affordance for . . . affordance itself, in other words, the form of a surface on which things are arranged, the way form comes to light [*mise en evidence*] and presence (to sit down at the table, to put something on the table, the negotiating table, the Holy Altar [*la Sainte Table*]).[5] This form gives sense or truth to the "table." One must thus understand that "sense or truth" (employed here as equivalents) are far from constituting simply the "intelligibility" of the sensible. At the same time, this intelligibility is nothing other than a more demanding, more intense grasp of sensible propriety itself. Or yet again, in distinguishing these two terms, one could say that the truth is the point or moment of interruption of the movement and opening up of sense. Interrupted, suspended, the drawing/design of sense [*le sens en son dess(e)in*] reveals at once its tracing out

6

[*tracé*] (its substance or bearing) and the truth, which is not its completion but, on the contrary, its very interruption.

It is for this reason that early on the word *drawing* took on, if not exactly the meaning, then the value associated with a sketch or a study. In *The Art of Painting*, Roger de Piles has a chapter "Of Designs," which begins: "The Designs, of which we intend to speak here, are the Thoughts that Painters commonly express on paper in order to execute the Work they are planning. One should number among Designs the studies made by the Great Masters, in other words, the Parts they have drawn after Nature, such as heads, hands, feet & entire Figures, Draperies, Animals, Trees, Plants, Flowers, and finally everything that enters into the Composition of a Painting [*Tableau*]. Because whether one considers it a good Design in relation to a Painting for which it is the Idea, or in relation to some Part for which it is a Study, it always deserves the attention of the Curious."[6]

(*Matter*—to recall a word that remains inseparable from "form"—is the name of form's resistance to its deformation. It is not a formless "content" that form comes to mold or model but rather the thickness, texture, and force of form itself. We will return to this claim later in order to understand how color and drawing are not as exterior to one another as might be thought, even as they remain irreducible and irreplaceable.)

Sketchbook 2

"With charcoal, he marked on the wall the ideas of things as they came to mind; it is customary for sharp and imaginative minds to pile up thought upon thoughts on the same subject."

—Chantelou, *Diary of the Cavaliere Bernini's Visit to France*

"DRAWING [*DESSEIN*], which signifies the goal, objective, end, and aim of action. But it also signifies a project, plan, or portrait of a few figures, the outline of a flat painting surface or relief that one wants to create: a common word amongst Painters, Statue makers, and other such artisans who draw or sketch."

—Antoine de Laval, *Drawings of Noble and Public Professions*

"On the difference between literature and painting with regard to the effect that can be produced by *the rough sketch of a thought*; in other words, on the impossibility, in literature, of making a sketch that will convey an idea to the mind, and of the strength with which an idea can be stated in the painter's rough sketch, or in his first draft. Music must be like literature, and I think that this difference between drawing and the other arts comes from the fact that in the latter, ideas are developed *in succession*, whereas the whole impression of a pictorial composition can be summed up in three or four lines.

. . . in painting, a fine indication, or a sketch infused with great feeling, can be equal in expression to the most finished production."

—Eugène Delacroix, *Journal*

"What is called 'good draftsmanship' is where nothing can be altered without destroying this inner life, regardless of whether this draftsmanship contradicts anatomy or botany or any other science."

—Wassily Kandinsky, *On the Spiritual in Art*

Formative Force

Drawing is therefore the Idea—it is the true form of the thing. Or more exactly, it is the gesture that proceeds from the desire to show this form and to trace it so as to show the form—but not to trace in order to reveal it as a form already received. Here, to trace is to find, and in order to find, to seek a form to come (or to let it seek and find itself)—a form to come that should or that can come through drawing.

In the sense of a project or intention, the *design* [dessein] to form or to show is originally only another word for drawing, which up until the eighteenth century was written in exactly the same way.[7] Both stem from *de-signare* (whence the Italian *disegno* and the today's *design*), of which we have conserved the term and notion *to designate*. Drawing designates the form or idea. It is the thought that designates, presents, monstrates, or ostentates. This signifies that it is not "demonstrative" thought—a demonstration does not show; it unfolds through stages, in such a way that it can be followed, accompanied, and even carried throughout its progression. Inversely, monstration puts one, as it were, before the fait accompli. But drawing's "fait accompli" is not simply that of the thing's monstration; it is the monstration of the form, idea, or thought, and thus of the thing as thought or thinkable—of the *ideated* [idéelle] thing, if one wants to distinguish between this word and *ideal*, to which it is perhaps too closely related. The ideated thing or the idea of the thing—the form—is not an ethereal image of the thing, nor is it how it appears. It is neither a noumenon nor a phenomenon. It is the thought of the thing, which is to say, its formation, re-formation, or transformation into truth. It is neither the generic notion of a "table" nor the real table on which I am writing but this drawing of a table—by Cézanne or Gropius—thanks to which a determinate thought is engendered or *forms itself*, distinct but not conceptual (although not rigorously perceptual per se and yet still *sensible*), precise and present but not proffered to any other use than that of thought, of the sensibility of thought.[8]

The same can be understood of industrial drawing, an architect or botanist's drawing as well as that of a painter or draftsman. Like all types of drawing that are assumed to be simply reproductive or imitative, even the first three categories mentioned here do not merely "reproduce" (what would a faithful and complete "reproduction" mean here?) but also always produce an idea, a thought, sense, or truth. The difference between these types of drawing and those qualified as artistic—a distinction that is initially difficult to maintain in any rigorous way—only resides in the mode of truth in play. There is a truth that is thought as conforming to a verifiable (identifiable, recognizable, or measurable) truth, and another that is thought as existing before a verification (in the literal sense of the term—as the production of the true), a truth that is not identifiable, recognizable or, even less, measurable—a truth first of all, and as a principle, unformed (for which, in consequence, a conformity cannot be given).

The thought of a non-conforming and unverifiable form, the thought of a form forming itself, of the self-formative form [*forme formatrice*]—in consequence, of the *formative force* of this very form, or again, of *the form in its force*, of the form or idea *as force*, in short, what the Greek call *dunamis*—is what constitutes the drawing of art or the art of drawing, this art, as we have already suggested, that constitutes the element, moment, or dimension not of formalized but formative, ostensive, and dynamic thought across all artistic fields. In fact, this triple qualification is to be understood not according to an additive but according to a synthetic mode: drawing creates this synthesis, and it is nothing other than the force of this ostensive formation. In still other terms, it is the gesture of putting something forth in its evidence. Or again, this is what Degas means when he is reported to have said: "Drawing is not the form, it is the manner of seeing the form." Or again, in quite different terms, what Armenini means when he writes in *On the True Precepts of Painting* from 1587: "Your drawing will be a pre-disposition which, first imagined in the mind then conceived by the soul and judgment, will finish by coming into existence in various modes on little pieces of paper."

The "manner" or "mode," as a property of the gesture of drawing, refers to nothing other than the singularity of form—and this singularity insofar as a truth, essence, or characteristic comes to light there (however one might want to phrase it), each time singular, unique, and exclusive to the drawn thing. It makes no essential difference whether this thing is reputed to correspond to the representation of a real object or whether it configures itself within itself without figuring anything; as a matter of fact, its *essence* consists entirely of the manner, mode, and allure of its gesture, the force of its movement, the weight and lightness of its mark [*trait*].

Sketchbook 3

"To draw is to outline an idea. The drawing is the clarification of thought. Through drawing, the sentiments and soul of the painter pass without difficulty into the mind of the viewer. A work without drawing is a house without a framework."

—Henri Matisse, *Writings on Art*

"The secret of the art of drawing is to discover within each object the specific manner in which a fluctuating line—which is its generative axis—expands out, like a wave that spreads out in ripples across the surface."

—Félix Ravaisson, *On the Teaching
of Drawing in Schools*

"The line shows first on an intact surface. A mark that carries its appearance to the end and only becomes interrupted after having circumscribed the surface at the precise point where the end cancels itself out in the beginning, it will be immediately a continuous line, the progressive exposure of a freedom, and at the same time the sensual pleasure [*jouissance*] of this freedom, as well as the desire to confound pleasure and freedom, to delimit their shared substance and their common subversion."

—René Char, "Search for the Base and the Summit"

"In its own way, drawing is the use of signs. Whoever draws with force, whoever inscribes on the unlimited depth of a sheet of paper his impression of a body, a city seen from afar, or a summit surrounded by clouds, only does this in distancing themselves from a line which evokes a head, house, or mountain drawn in a conventional way."

—Yves Bonnefoy, *The Wandering Life*

"The nascent form is an unspoken reality on the way to becoming manifest for the first time. . . . The represented objects serve to manifest their own movement of appearance: their function is to anticipate themselves or to surface before what they appear to be."

—Max Loreau, *Of Creation*

"Maybe the most important word is the word *tension*. Lines shouldn't . . . even vibrate anymore, be able to anymore."

—Pablo Picasso, *Writings on Art*

The Pleasure of Drawing

Due to its nature, no doubt, drawing is represented, experienced, and experimented with as a compulsion, like the effect of an irresistible impetus. Valéry writes that drawing constitutes "perhaps the strongest temptation of the mind," and a number of painter's lives show a precocious and often overwhelming compulsion to scribble, draft, trace, sketch out, or outline (right up to the "priapism of drawing" to which Greuze refers when speaking of Saint-Aubin).[9]

A phrase by Vasari about the young Michelangelo summarizes what he and other authors of the "lives" of painters repeat about so many other artists, sometimes with abundant detail: "His genius led him to the pleasure of drawing; furtively, he spent as much time at it as he could, for which his father and elders scolded him."

One could certainly ask if this disposition or impulse [*pulsion*] really can be attributed to the future artist in question, or whether it stems from a well-rehearsed topos, whose initial model is found, no doubt, in the story of the young Giotto, who drew while tending a flock. But the very invention of this topos ought to be questioned: whether originating in reality or not, why should drawing receive this singular treatment that makes it the model of art ingenuously engendered from its own genius?

Be that as it may, this characteristic obsessive disposition is not specific to budding artists; it is one of the most widely shared dispositions among young children before the intervention of other motor schemes, such as more technical manipulations (construction, assembly) or writing. It is not by chance that early humanity has left us testimonies of intense drawing activity—tracings, engravings, graffiti or scratches, hand-drawn lines, scorings of figures, rhymes, outlines, or incisions.

Of course, we should not mistake the fact that the nature of these traces has been conserved for us in visible and tangible ways, even if we are forever deprived of the songs and dances that undoubtedly accompanied them. But we should think here beyond empirical reasoning; with our ancestor's drawings, it is the essence of a formative force—at once musical, choreographic, chromatic, and poetic—that is inscribed and transmitted to us, like the inaugural gesture of a monstration through which man has drawn himself and destined himself. One could even say—destined himself to draw (himself), to renew and multiply without end the sketch that man is.

And yet, it should be admitted that *pleasure* is an ambiguous word whose meaning errs on the side of complacency and satisfaction, of facility and lack of exigency, just as it can remain open to a joy or sensual pleasure [*jouissance*] whose open-endedness, excess, and insatiety are its true condition. We will return to this, but one should at once emphasize that such an opposition remains too crude when stated in this way. It is a matter of identifying polarities and not of opposing a contemptible repletion and a sublime exaltation. In truth, the ambiguity of the word *pleasure* is also its resource—without allowing for any dichotomy, it is capable of combining the value of charm and that of anticipation or aspiration with extreme delicacy. As distinguished from a fulfillment of a need, pleasure comprises a renewed dynamic, revived by the desire to which it responds—something like what René Char called "the realized love of desire still desiring" ("The Formal Share"). In his own way, Gilles Deleuze affirms: "pleasure comes to interrupt desire's positivity," and thus it is "the only means for a person or subject to 'recover themselves' [*s'y retrouver*] within a process that overwhelms them."[10] But one could say that it is precisely not a question of "recovering oneself"; the subject is overwhelmed in pleasure as well, providing that it is not sought, thought, or received as a normative "satisfaction." More exactly, it overwhelms itself, or it is "subject" in and as excess of itself [*il est 'sujet' comme débordement de soi*].

Thus, when Adorno in the introduction to *Aesthetic Theory* opposes the vision of art as "sensual pleasure" with such vehemence, declaring, "the more works of art are understood, the less one finds pleasure,"[11] his entire claim illustrates quite clearly that what he calls "sensual pleasure" is a consumptive, bourgeois satisfaction that loathes the attitude he describes with the words *admiration* and *contemplation.* For admiration and contemplation—which in fact is not the worst way to name the relation that is best suited to the work of art—are a form of pleasure, but a pleasure that is not satisfied by grasping an object: it satisfies itself in transporting a subject outside itself. Hegel says this quite simply: "works of art are not made to be consumed." Contemplation does not consume what it contemplates—through contemplation, it renews its hunger and thirst.

Sketchbook 4

"Drawing is possession. To each line must correspond another line that balances it just as one grasps it, possessing it with two hands.

—Henri Matisse, *Writings on Art*

"Bassetti often repeated a scarcely obeyed maxim during his time—that painting should not be exercised daily like a mechanical art; rather, the painter should only start working when he feels animated by a gentle pleasure that draws him to work."

—Stendhal, *The Italian Schools of Painting*

"Just as my pleasure is born of affection, so is affection born of beauty. Thus it may still be said that beauty is the cause of my pleasure . . . the love that springs from the outward bodily beauty that we see will doubtless give far greater pleasure to him who appreciates it more than to him who appreciates it less. This is why I think Apelles took far greater pleasure in contemplating

Campaspe's beauty than Alexander the Great did . . . and perhaps it was partly on this account that Alexander the Great resolved to give her to him who seemed fitted to appreciate her most perfectly."

—Baldassare Castiglione, *The Book of the Courtier*

"It is drawing which values precision—every stroke is explicit and ambiguous—yet it has totally forgotten itself in its openness to what it has met. And the meeting is so close you can't tell whose trace is whose. A map of love indeed."

—John Berger, *The Shape of a Pocket*

"Joy and a way of being open to art and the beautiful, but not as pleasure or self- satisfaction resulting from its own virtues."

—Emmanuel Levinas, *Outside the Subject*

Forma Formans

Homo, animal monstrans—animal designans. This *designation* responds to what our culture calls *mimesis*. Mimesis is neither a copy nor an imitation that reproduces. It reproduces, in the sense that it produces the form (i.e., the idea or truth of the thing) again—in other words, like new—which is also to say, indissociably, it re-produces the emotion by which this truth not only distinguishes itself but also marks, imprints, and makes itself.

To be sure, *mimesis* is no less dependent on a system of simple reproduction. Once the gods possess entirely human bodies and once the actions of heroes become the actions of men, it becomes a question of "imitating," just as musical rhythms and tones are grounded in human passions. What is imitated, however, is not given with sensation or perception. What mimesis must take hold of and make evident, what it must show or present, is nothing other than the Idea. It would not be out of place to say that drawing manifests or puts to work the very design [*dessein*] of mimesis—the formative and rousing force of the Idea, the ostention and emotion of truth.

This also amounts to saying that the form that drawing draws—the form it traces, opens, and designates—is essentially valuable as a formative force, prior to any other determination or quality, and so prior to being, in a sense, a *beautiful form*. *Forma formans* more than *forma formata*. If, in a general manner, drawing can find its worth as an element or dimension common to all aesthetic fields, it is because what one calls "aesthetic" concerns a "feeling" [*sentir*] (*aisthanonmai*), not as a sensory faculty that records information but a *sensing* [ressentir], in other words, a faculty of making sense, or of letting it be formed. The sense formed cannot be exhausted by any sensoriality or sensibility but, on the contrary, exhausts and exceeds them in drawing them to the limit of their potential intensity. "To sense" [*ressentir*] is to receive a sense (to receive and give, indiscernibly), the sense or value of a sensation. One might add—to feel without sensing, as in the simple perception of data (a smooth surface, the noise of a car, etc.) is not to *feel* [sentir] in the strict sense but only to take note. Drawing also *notes*, whether through traced, musical, dance, or filmic notations. But it does not "take" note. It does not record, or it does not settle for "taking note." The word *note*, which stems from the notion of a known or situated object, can have two meanings—either fixed and identifiable information or an opening and sketch leading toward that which does not become information but a sense.

It is this *sense* that can be called "Idea," "thought," or "form." It is this *sense* (or rather, once again and indistinguishably, this truth) that is designated and drawn, this sense that forms the entire design of what is named by an enigmatic and sometimes confusing term: *art*. Its enigma arises from the way in which what it "designates" is neither what is "already designated" (or already drawn, already formed, conformed, and noted) nor even the "designatable." What it designs to designate is exactly the *drawing of the nascent form whose form is nowhere given in advance.*

In other terms, drawing unfolds a novel sense that does not conform to a pre-formed project. It is carried away by a *design* that joins with the movement, gesture, and expansion of the mark [*trait*].[12] Its pleasure is the sensual pleasure [*jouissance*] of this unfolding, or the pleasure of this unfolding itself inasmuch as it invents, finds, and summons itself further, projected onto the trace that has nevertheless not preceded it.

What matters to drawing, what carries it and carries it away and gives it its impulse and mark [*trait*], is this birth—its event, force, and form insofar as it finds itself *in statu formandi*. "To draw" is at once to give birth to form—to *give* birth in *letting* it be born—and thus to show it, to bring it to light [*mettre en évidence*]—or rather, and here again, to allow its evidence to offer and dispose itself.

Sketchbook 5

"I have no need to deform. I start out from the formless and I form."

—Georges Braque, *Day and Night*

"Because it forms anew arising from itself all the formations given as models, it is in each of its aspects form *ab initio*, underivable *novum*, and absolute beginning."

—Werner Hamacher, *"Parusie, Mauern"*

"Ingres used to say to his students: 'Gentlemen, everything has a form, even smoke.'"

—Felix Bracquemond, *Of Drawing and Color*

"When drawing pursues its own adventure, it breaks little by little with the ties that subject it to the empire of forms. It opens itself, dazzling in the pithy threshold of the instant. Its movement springs forth, interrupts itself, starting again in order to intercept the flight that the line, turning in contour, threatens to efface. It is against its dissolution in form that drawing unleashes itself [*se déchaîne*]"

—Luc Richir, "Drawing"

"The question of drawing differs significantly from the question of *Hamlet*. It does not ask: 'To be or not to be' but 'to be and not to be.' This is the reason for the fundamental fragility of drawing—not a clear alternative between to be and not to be but a somber and paradoxical conjunction between being and not being."

—Alain Badiou, "Drawing"

"In a drawing, each mark [*trait*] belongs to the whole of space and conspires with all others in the rhythm of empty and full spaces, before elucidating any figurative proposition. The 'formal dimension' is the dimension according to which form forms itself, in other words, its rhythmic dimension."

—Henri Maldiney, *Art: The Illumination of Being*

"Even when one sees something and draws it, one reflects on 'how-to-draw,' on the small points, for example, the small brackets, the stains, the lines, the curves, and so on."

—Georg Baselitz, *What You Are Not Is a Self-Portrait*

From Self Toward Self

But in this intimate combination of the two gestures of birth and ostension, the one can never separate from the other—birth cannot simply remain an interminable process (a mark must be traced), nor can ostension simply present a formed or closed form. The *status nascendi* or *status formandi*—this *status* that has no stable state and that remains incessantly metastable—never stops preceding and extending itself beyond itself. It began "before" and it will continue "after" what allows itself to be identified as the present of its presentation. Formed form summons a new formation; the Idea makes demands on itself [*se demande elle-même*] beyond its identifications; thought proves to be that of a desire always opened up again, because the truth of the thing cannot be presented once and for all, given that to present it—to form it—is already to remove a part of its own capacity for opening, forming, transforming, or deforming. The possibilities of truth are infinite, and it is this infinity that thought designs.[13] Drawing carries out the gesture of its desire. Think of all that has been drawn that we name "hand" or "circle," and everything for which we have no name, which are allures, inflexions, intervals, bearings, flux, torsions, and so on. It is always a matter of the desire to form an additional truth, or if one prefers, to form an additional sense whose "final" truth is only ever the interruption and suspension at the edge of the work.

In taking shape [*en se dessinant*], this desire reveals itself to be pleasure. Not the pleasure of completion but the pleasure of tension. In effect, it is not only a need extended toward the aim of satisfaction or achievement. In desire, completion and conclusion can only come in a provisional and closed manner (what one calls "the work" in the most common meaning of the term). Beyond all need and all aim, desire makes repeated demands on itself [*se redemande lui-même*]—its design is nothing other than an intensification and a limitless differentiation or dissemination. The first person who drew on a rock face a deer, his own hand, or a sinuous line opened the door to an endlessly modulated repetition of his gesture and to an unlimited variation on his theme. This repetition, for which drawing constitutes the opening and strange necessity, nurtures a pleasure whose essence is repetition itself. From here it becomes possible to understand that art, in all fields, cannot be separated from pleasure.[14]

As previously stated, it is necessary simultaneously to distinguish and to conjoin the two possible values of "pleasure." It is either satisfaction, in which desire fades away, or it is desire itself, which takes pleasure in its own intensity. One could even say it in these terms: either a pleasure of charm or a pleasure of attraction; either a pleasure of repletion or a pleasure of seduction; either a lowering of tension or an intensity that makes itself necessary again [*se redemande*]; either a contentment (and with it the finished form) or a contention (and with it, infinitely, the force of a new formation).

If it is certainly not possible to separate one type of pleasure from another without further ado (if it is not even possible to determine to what extent there are two variants of *one* pleasure or two *separate* kinds of pleasure)—there will always occur a necessary release or an exacting revival—it is nevertheless not possible to overlook that the gesture of art in general, and of drawing in particular, does not aim for the repletion or discharge of a tension but rather the opening and revival or resurgence of an intensity. The satisfaction of the work is only as such a moment-limit of art. Whether this might be in the work of the artist or in the behavior (taste and judgment) of the connoisseur, it concerns a prolonged intensity, whose "satisfaction" cannot be expressed insofar as it does not become exhausted in entropy and insofar as, on the contrary, it opens onto what Blanchot terms the unworking [*désœuvrement*] of the work.

In a wider sense, one could say that pleasure is nothing other than self-affection (stated briefly, the relation to the self, the subject, or the becoming-subject) of a "repeated self-questioning" [*un "se redemander"*] or of a "renewed self-desiring," while displeasure is the self-affection of "self-withdrawal" [*un "'se repousser"*]. To speak of self-affection is to speak of what does not arise only as an incidental and accidental affection. It is to speak of what in effect arises (as incident and/or accident) to the subject as that which makes it subject, which relates the subject to itself. It is by affecting oneself, desiring or withdrawing from oneself [*se repoussant*], or pleasing oneself in this desire or displeasing oneself in this refusal, that the "self" is formed or the "self" is made [*qu'il "se" forme ou qu'il "se" fait*], in other words, that a "self," a "to self," manifests or overcomes itself [*survient ou se survient*]. Manifesting itself, in this way the subject comes to distance itself from its self and can experience pleasure or pain, in other words, the expansion or retraction of its being.

We are not speaking here of psychology. We are speaking of that for which sentiment or passion in their diverse forms are only colorations and modulations, but which deep down is only existence extended toward itself or turned against itself. Desire—with its pleasure and/or pain—is not the subject's response to an object (given or lacking); it is above all else a response or reflection [*renvoi*] of being to being itself. It is the referring [*envoi*] of being to itself, in other words, precisely what *is* not but refers itself [*s'envoie*] toward itself, which seeks itself and wants itself [*se veut*], whose being exists in this tension of self toward self, and whose formula—implicating a hiatus [*écart*] between self and self, a hiatus endlessly taken up again and revived—summons an incessant overcoming. Not a "satisfaction" but an "un-satisfaction" that always transports itself further. What one calls "art" is the knowledge of such a passion [*emportement*].

Sketchbook 6

"[As when two mirrors face each other] the eye transmits through the atmosphere its own image to all the objects that are in front of it and receives them into itself, that is to say on its surface, whence they are taken in by the common sense, which considers them and, if they are pleasing, commits them to memory."

—Leonardo Da Vinci, *Notebooks*

"By feeling oneself enshrouded in papers that speak, I mean drawings, sketches, memories . . . one may enjoy oneself completely."

—Eugène Delacroix, *Journal*

"The art of drawing, the Holy Covenant on which everything depends."

—Degas's father to his son

"I renew for you the assurance of my constant love of drawing."

—Edgar Degas to a correspondent

"Drawing allows you to gather sensibility's fast movement, its disentangling beyond the hindrance of matter or painting. The sign no longer encounters obstacles but, on the contrary, enables images that do not dramatize their own appearance but render it agile and spontaneous."

—Achille Bonito Oliva,
The Italian Trans-Avant-Garde

"I think only of the joy of seeing the sun rise once more and of being able to work a little bit, even under difficult conditions."

—Henri Matisse, *Writings on Art*

"I draw—This line will not enclose or surround an emptiness. A trace extended from a body's wake and its breathing, this will be a sign chosen from a thousand others but it will assume them all."

—André Masson, *The Pleasure of Painting*

"Man does not like to dwell with himself; nevertheless he loves; it is necessary then that he seek elsewhere something to love. He can find it only in beauty."

—Blaise Pascal, *Discourse on the Passion of Love*

Consenting to Self

There is no art without pleasure. This does not mean that art is foreign to strain, anxiety, or pain in all values of the word. But it does mean that art always proceeds from a tension that searches for itself [*se recherche*], that enjoys reaching out, not in order to reach the goal of relaxation but to renew this tension infinitely, which also means that pleasure's (ex)tension carries with it displeasure, or that this distinction itself is blurred.

The emotion to which we have previously referred is none other than that by which tension *forms itself*, just as form reaches out, extends, erects, and projects itself [*se bande et s'élance*]. This emotion gives the sense of the form that feels itself forming and opening—to nothing other than itself, to its own sense of form, to the sensation, sentiment, and consent of the movement that receives and approves itself and that makes repeated demands on itself [*se redemande*] at its own birth.

The pleasure of drawing plays out in this assent, in this consent toward the self of a movement whose most fundamental law is a fidelity to itself and to its own impulse—to its thought and emotion, and not to the reproduction of a given form.[15] The pleasure of drawing is the pleasure of those who do not acknowledge any given form. One could even say, of those who do not acknowledge any form but who find themselves in the world as if the first form had just come to distinguish itself in the motion of its tracing out [*tracé*]. At the same time, if this form opens space in delimiting—in delineating—areas, it is nevertheless not satisfied with separating, as one says sometimes too exclusively of the line [*trait*]. (Heinrich Wölfflin distinguishes in this way the "linear" from the "painterly."[16]) The form that draws itself *shares* space in all senses of the word: it divides it, it spreads it out and connects it with volume and depth; it lets in its resonance and pulse, tonalities and color.

Insofar as this consent toward self consents to an impulse and not a given, to a birth and not a figure, it consents to an outside, to an other—to an alterity or alteration that, before all beginnings, will have mobilized the gesture without pre-scribing [*prédessiner*] or predestining it but tracing out [*frayant*] a path—opening up an attraction, an appeal that precedes the mark [*une attirance, un attrait avant le trait*], the pleasure of a desire.

"Consent toward self" could be a formula for the pleasure specific to art or even, perhaps, to pleasure in general—to pleasure and, indissociably, to the exigency and effort that are necessary to it. If, in texts and discourses on artistic practices, emphasis is most frequently placed on work, pain, sweat, and anxiety, it is perhaps due to the domination of hard work as a value in modern culture, but it is also certainly due to the effectiveness [*effectivité*] of hard work that art demands—in other words, the *ars*, *technē,* and mechanisms of production that give their all, art's means and ends, bereft as it is of any natural engendering. (In fact, it follows that the "imitation of nature" has never truly been anything other than the imitation of the inimitable forming force of a germination or of a reproduction and growth presumed without art, in other words, without artifice and thus without search or effort.) The fact remains that these same texts—or even more so, those that take the viewpoint of ends that are sought and of the work's reception—never fail to mention "pleasure." (Grace, charm, success, finesse, magic, rapture, delicacy, or force, and finally beauty itself or sublimity, among numerous other terms, cannot be dissociated from pleasure, however complex or subtle it might be.) When one speaks of an artist at work, love, pleasure, and joy are never effaced by work but rather only modulated and rendered nobler.

There is a remarkable passage in which Félibien places in a mise en abime the pleasure taken in seeing the representation of passions in painting; the same pleasure is in turn considered a passion, inasmuch as it communicates from the soul to the body its specific effect, comparable to the blossoming [*éclosion*] of a flower, an "outward appearance" that doubles the passion formed by painting:

> "Since we chance upon the discourse of the passions, I beg you not to be weary of reporting everything you have observed about it."

"In effect," I responded, "it is such a necessary & such a considerable part of painting that I do not believe one can say anything more important, & which gives you more pleasure when you will see a few paintings [*tableaux*] where the passions have been well represented."

"Considering the very pleasure that I already receive from painting," Pymander says, "shouldn't you be speaking about a passion?"

"Yes, without doubt," I respond, "if it is true that pleasure is formed in the soul through the presence of objects which gives us joy. It is this joy that makes the heart open out, like a flower which blossoms [*éclot*], which creates a smile, which is only the effect & outward appearance of an interior passion."[17]

Sketchbook 7

"How a figure merits no praise if its attitude does not express the passions of the soul."

—Leonardo da Vinci, *Notebooks*

"Seeing one of the local painters who was painting a shrine for a peasant, Andrea, who had never seen anything of the kind before, was seized by a sudden marvel . . . and there came to him a very great desire and so violent a love for that art, that without losing time he began to scratch drawings of animals and figures on walls and stones with pieces of charcoal or with the point of his knife, in so masterly a manner that it caused no small marvel to all who saw them."

—Giorgio Vasari, *Life of Andrea del Castagno*

"'Art lies hidden within nature; he who can rest it from her, has it.' 'Wrest' here means to draw out the rift and to draw the design with the drawing-pen on the drawing-board."

—Martin Heidegger, *Origin of the Work of Art*

". . . avoiding if not the influence of a drawing (a line "willingly grasping"), at least its insistence, the weight within it of an intention or even a phantasm. A good mark [*trait*] does not press a hand to the paper; on the contrary, it allows the hand to touch the paper lightly, as if raising into the air in 'levitation,' and establishing around the drawn figure 'a sort of haze of interpretation.' So what exactly is this contact between pencil and paper? An exchange of gentleness, like a caress or a taking flight. From which we find such a precise and exquisite metaphor: 'the wax (from the pencil), soft substance, adheres to the miniscule bumps of the graphic field, and it is the trace of this 'nimble flight of bees' which creates the line. . . .' The wax (literal) of the pencil that draws, and the honey (figural) to be produced from the gold carried away by bees—the imagination closes the circle of a single nimble animality in on itself."

—Jean-Pierre Richard, *Roland Barthes,*
Last Landscape

"There is one Thing, which is as the Salt of a Drawing [*Desseins*], and which I can't express better than by the Word *Character*. This Character consists then in the manner in which the Painter thinks Things. 'Tis the seal that distinguishes his Works from those of other Men, and which he imprints on these Works like the lively Image of his Mind."

—Roger de Piles, *The Idea of the Perfect Painter*

Gestural Pleasure

That classical aesthetics was an aesthetics of pleasure should not lead us to believe that pleasure has no place outside aesthetics. In truth, no aesthetics is exempt from a pleasure principle (whether related or not to Freud's "pleasure principle," which indeed we will have to address). Provided that one takes care to distinguish satisfaction—and even more, contentment, repletion, and relaxation—from the pleasure of desire, from an intensity that seeks itself and revives itself, one cannot fail to discern this pleasure, however dissimulated it might have become beneath technical, signifying, political, or philosophical theories. One would no longer speak of art without speaking of a certain attraction [*attrait*]—that of the artists for their art, that of the spectator for this same art in the work of art, and more subtly but no doubt more truly, that which the work takes in itself, which draws it out and opens it, which extends it beyond its achievement, and which is most specifically this infinite, inconclusive pleasure toward which the artist's desire strives, and our desire thanks to his.[18]

This pleasure is inconclusive because it is in essence the pleasure of beginning, of an opening, and so the pleasure of a desire that is aimed less toward an object to be attained than toward this very opening, toward its impulse, toward its own possibility. This possibility appears not in terms of representable, calculable, and realizable "possibles" but as the indeterminate possibility of the possible as such, of a potentiality to exist [*pouvoir-être*] that is not the still-abstract form of an incarnate being—this possible of which Bergson says that it is only ever the retrospective projection based on the real (as if I were to say that Géricault's *Centaur Kidnapping a Nymph* was possible by the mere fact that the painter had drawn it) but which is itself a modality and consistence of being—a being of power, an *energeia* of *dunamis* in Aristotle's words, the reality of an impetus, of birth, of beginning.

This means: formation understood not as a simple anteriority and as a process determinable from its causes—the principal being its final cause, the intended goal, the form represented as achieved (to speak again in Aristotle's terms)—but formation thought in terms of efficacy, of the truth and sense of the form *that forms itself*, in the act, force [*puissance*] and tension of its *self-forming* [son se-former] (one could say "informing" itself in the double meaning of [dis]covering itself, learning itself, and putting itself into form, conforming itself to this "self" that formation, at the same time, discovers and lets come into being).

The ordering of causes completely withdraws here. It is not that it is suppressed. No doubt a final cause subsists—a "model," as it were, or an "idea" in the sense of a regulative representation—just as other causes subsist (i.e., material, efficient, formal causes, with the understanding that the last often overlaps with a final cause)—but the gesture of the artist is no longer governed by causes. The gesture for which drawing offers us the essence and excellence—for which it proposes what we should call the *drawing* (the sketch, the project, the process), but which belongs just as well to the dancer, musician, or filmmaker—this gesture is above all what is most proper to a *gesture*: an immanent *signifiance*,[19] in other words, without the sign taking off toward the signified, but a sense that is offered right at the body [*à même le corps*], right at a body that becomes less active, efficient, or operative than the body that gives itself over to a motion—to an *e*motion—that receives it, coming from beyond its functional corporeality. This gestural body is different from the organic body, without being a body without organs.[20] Rather, it becomes the body-*organon* of art, and thus of the technique (*ars*—*technē*) that is in play, whether graphic, vocal or colored, tactile or verbal.

And so it goes for each gesture of application. Neither engineer, nor athlete, nor farmer is content simply to carry out the successive steps of a plan given in advance. No *design* is resolved in the (re)production of a rigorously established *drawing*. Conversely, no *drawing* is limited to the simple transcription of the *design* from which it originates. But the difference that is proper to art—the difference of the gesture that draws for the "pleasure" of drawing—is made when the *design* incorporates into its own intention a dimension that exceeds the intention: a tension that allows the form to open itself to its own formation, whatever the idea, aim, or end given. In every form of art, something plays itself out that in other contexts one calls *gestural pleasure*.

Matisse writes: "You should always follow the desire of the line, the point where it wishes to enter or die away."

In art, it is a question of this disposition to "follow." This disposition neither invalidates nor replaces any work, project, or calculation, but without it every project remains projection, and all calculation remains computation. The passivity implicated in this "following" is that of opening up to the distinctive and singular event of an impetus, motion, line, or emotion. One can (and often one must) refuse to speak of "genius," "inspiration," and "creation." The fact remains that "art" (whose name must also remain problematic, even suspect) never takes place without this moment of "following," without this openness to chance or "happiness" (in the sense in which one says "bliss of expression" [*bonheur d'expression*])—and consequently, to a pleasure or joy—that constitutes "the line" itself, its birth between hand and paper, under pencil or pen, in such a way that knowledge and know-how, with all their intentions, also know at the same time how to be led by this line that still does not yet exist, by this form in the process of forming itself.

Here Duchamp's motif of the *rendez-vous* best reveals its truth for all types of artistic gesture and for all periods. In effect, it is not the *ready-made* alone that proceeds from a *"rendez-vous"* (a *rendez-vous* that nobody schedules or makes but rather that grips whoever encounters something there . . . a line, an inflection, a nuance, an allure).

In addition, one should acknowledge that the "line" we have been referring to initially in terms of the visual or graphic arts belongs in other sensible forms to all artistic domains—melodic line, architectural, choreographic, or filmic line, and so on. Following Kandinsky, we should also add line and point and plane, given his proposal for an aesthetic transversality of drawing's elements.[21] (However, what Kandinsky believed reducible to a single graphic notion must, on the contrary, be thought as an irreducible plurality. There are as many "lines," "points," and "planes" as there are specific sensible modalities, which is also to say, forms of sensibility, and there is never anywhere a general sensibility—in essence, *aisthesis* is differential.)

What traverses these differences, without acquiring any proper form, is a sensible setting into motion [*ébranlement*] and the birth or rising of form, a formation that takes pleasure in itself by the way it comes. What differentiates itself is *sensing* [*sentir*] itself, which does not exist as such but rather as the dual difference between sensed and sensing, on the one hand, and the modes of sensing, on the other. *Sensing*—in other words, *sense* in the fullest extent of the term—thrusts open that through which all relations and distinctions are opened. It is the impulse and pulse of being in the world, and all senses, sentiments, sensitivities, and sensualities are delineations of this impulse and pulse—taken up again in order to be more finely and intensely *drawn*, carried toward an infinite force [*puissance*] across what we call the "arts."

There is no mystery in this, or rather, there is only what the word *mystery* properly designates—that which illuminates by itself, what resorts to no reason outside itself. Such is the specific pleasure we are speaking about—the pleasure of making oneself available to this chance, which is the chance and risk of existence, or the pleasure of a certain abandon, surrendering to grace. Indeed, how else could we otherwise name this preference given to a mastery (a technique or an art) that is capable of giving itself over to a movement that exceeds it without effacing it?

Sketchbook 8

"Upon each leaf it is
a pattern more
of logic than a purpose
links each part to the rest,

   . . .

Under the leaf, the same
though the smooth green
is gone. Now the ribbed
Design—if not
the purpose, is explained."

—William Carlos Williams,
"The Crimson Cyclamen"

"The mark's grace signifies that at the origin of *graphein* there is debt or gift rather than a representational fidelity."

—Jacques Derrida, *Memoirs of the Blind*

"Each line is inhabited by its own history, it does not explain, it is the event of its own materialization."

—Cy Twombly

"The mark interrupts itself in the instant it is achieved."

—André du Bouchet, *Of a Line That*
Figures and Disfigures

"At nightfall, observe the faces of men and women in the street—what grace and gentleness they reveal."

—Leonardo da Vinci, *Notebooks*

"Sometimes it is the bear that invents art, by scratching on walls and leaving furrows, which his human companion . . . demarcates with surprise, with fear, and with the desire to give them more visibly the mysterious feature he finds in them. Sometimes, like Leonardo da Vinci, man looks at the stones and the walls, recognizes in them spots that are figures, that appear through slight modification. Sometimes he lets his dirty fingers drag along the surface of the rocks—or on himself—and these traces please him, and the mud is already color. Sometimes, finally, the one who breaks the bone or the stone with which to arm himself, also breaks it apart for his own delight, perfects these useless fragments, believes he makes the pieces more effective because of certain happy features he inscribes in them."

—Maurice Blanchot, *Friendship*

"Drawing extends the act of the hand, and with it the wrist, the forearm, the gaze, and finally the whole body. Against the intellectualizing to which we have wanted to reduce it sometimes, drawing produces a rhythmic configuration of the real born from the very rhythm of the body."

—Daniel Arasse, "The Memory of Drawing"

The Form-Pleasure

To address more directly the pleasure at issue, let us draw on an analysis from Freud's work on the subject of aesthetic form. What is at issue is in no way a question of entering into a psychoanalysis of art. On the contrary. But it happens that Freud—as we will see, in spite of himself—offers us an invaluable resource.[22]

Freud establishes at the least a parallel, and at the most a continuity, between sexual pleasure and aesthetic pleasure (as we will see, indecision on this point stems from the underlying difficulty that he encounters). (Meaning at least—let us note in passing—that for Freud, it is obvious that aesthetics is a matter of pleasure. It should be reiterated that this assumption is not open to debate, on the condition that we agree on what "pleasure" means).

The central element of this proximity between sexual and aesthetic pleasure—once again, analogical, or genealogical, or perhaps both—is found in the articulation of two types of pleasure, or rather, of two moments of the same pleasure (this further hesitation also sends us to the heart of the problem) within a process involved in the lowering and ultimate release of a tension. On the sexual level,[23] the first type of pleasure plays itself out across the progression of the scene of seduction, from outward attraction right up to genital orgasm. This progression brings into play three simultaneous processes, which are related to one another as in a contrapuntal relation—it retraces the path of the stages of sexual development from childhood to adulthood; it traverses different regimes of the sensible (sight, hearing, smell, touch); and it moves along the body, turning it into a succession of erogenous zones (Freud specifies that all parts of the body can assume this quality), right up to concentration on the privileged zone where orgasm can take place.

The intertwining of stages, sensorial regimes, and zones acts as a combination whose ensemble composes at once a finalized process (through access to genital satisfaction, the relaxation and dissolution of forms) and a mode of autonomous functioning in which the inherent qualities of the sensible multiplicity are in themselves brought or brought back into play (particularly by untying the body from a perceptive integration turned toward ends in order to hand it over to a pure sensation of the self as body in the world, as body toward the other, as body to body). If the tension that characterizes the finalized process may be characterized as pleasure (which is not in principle a property of tension, as Freud specifies) this is both because it clears the way to the final relaxation and because this opening itself is made possible by the playing out of a sensibility that exists in itself, released from its operative or informative finalities—in other words, a sensuality, if it is true that beneath this term we understand a sensibility that exists in itself.

It is for this reason that Freud can write that the ensemble of stages belongs legitimately to sexual phenomenon, while the fixation exclusive to one of these stages (to vision alone, for example, or to a single zone apart from the genitals), stems from perversion, in other words, from the diversion [*détournement*] of the sexual purpose.[24] We will not enter into these problems here except to point to the fact that all Freudian analysis thus rests on a double principal—that of a normative completion, in relation to which the rest is subordinate and instrumental, and that of a relatively autonomous valorization of assumedly preparatory elements and moments. Of course, the entire interpretive decision depends *in fine* on how to understand the expression "relatively autonomous." This expression does not come from Freud. It goes without saying that for him the purposiveness [*finalité*] of "terminal" pleasure largely dominates the whole, and that, in general, Freudian pleasure has an end, in other words, a goal and end term ("discharge" or relaxation). As we will see, what remains important for aesthetic reflection is that, in spite of everything, Freud himself foregrounds the importance of the constitution of sensibility in sensuality, because what characterizes "fore-pleasure" [*plaisir préliminaire*] can be designated as sensuality, if by this word one understands a sensibility that pleasures itself [*jouit d'elle-même*] and is not content with providing sensorial information. Aesthetic pleasure is nothing other than sensuality communicating itself to everyone (or tending to do so) and obtaining pleasure from this communication.[25]

Sexual or aesthetic, and probably more sexual *and* aesthetic, this sensuality takes pleasure in tension, in its own tension felt not as the lack of an object but as an expansion of a subject. This sensuality gives itself *pleasure desiring*, as Lacan says in commenting on Freud: "The paradox of . . . fore-pleasures [*plaisirs préliminaires*] is precisely that they persists in opposition to the purposes of the pleasure principle. It is only insofar as the pleasure of desiring, or, more precisely, the pleasure of experiencing unpleasure, is sustained that we can speak of the sexual valorization of the preliminary stages of the act of love."[26]

To be sure, in order to be as thorough as possible, we would have to analyze more closely how the normativity of a "discharge" is also tied for Freud to procreation, even if in a less direct and evident manner. Because if it remains true that Freud keeps procreation on the horizon without really explaining what this horizon is, it is no less true that the conjunction (at least up until today) of man's procreation with a sexuality largely independent of procreation (i.e., not subjected to the *œstrus*, as Freud emphasizes) demands particular attention. Here is not the place to dwell on this issue, even if the relation between this question and the question of art should also be considered.

But what should hold our attention is the Freudian analogy between sexual pleasure and aesthetic pleasure. When Freud studies the latter (in *The Joke and Its Relation to The Unconscious*), it passes through a deliberate reference to what *Three Essays on the Theory of Sexuality* developed apropos of sexual pleasure. In effect, Freud posits an analogy between "fore-pleasure" and aesthetic form, qualified as "a pleasure premium" (*Lustprämie*). The same "premium" constitutes gratification from seduction, through which the joking form [*forme plaisante*] (to be specific, a witty remark) opens a path to the expression of a libidinal or aggressive impulse, in an operation whose aim is orgasm. Thus, aesthetic form assumes the preparatory and mediatory quality that, in the sexual order, is that of sexual behavior.

We can draw three conclusions from Freud's argument [*dispositif*] as we have briefly summarized it.

1. The first (which is the most widely recognized in studies on Freud and art) consists in noticing the general impossibility for Freud to consider aesthetic form or art as legitimate in their own right. We already know that Freud himself recognizes this impossibility, and this comes from someone who declares that artists know more than psychoanalysis on the subject of the human soul. If we try to circumscribe it, the nature of this "knowledge" must not be separated from "aesthetic form." In other words, this *form* is itself—or rather, it possesses or proceeds from—a *force* of the soul's penetration, capture, or transport. To speak this way requires no dubious exaltations—it simply concerns the movement in which the possibility of *designating* a world is *animated*, when before there would only have been milieus and interactions. Freud is right—art holds over us a knowledge that exceeds all other, and this knowledge is conformed like drawing, not like language.

2. The second conclusion allows us to state that the pleasure of form—in a certain manner doubly diminished by Freud as the pleasure of tension (which, for Freud, is painful) and as simple preparation—precisely constitutes for him aesthetic pleasure, and on two counts: on the one hand, pleasure as such is designated as "aesthetic," and on the other, sexual response is nothing other than the pleasure of the senses considered in themselves. Everything happens as if Freud recalls the proper sense of the Greek *aesthesis* ("sensation"), while inversely he seeks an aestheticization, at best allusive and indirect, of the sexual relation in light of what he designates as the preliminary pleasure in this relation. As it happens, if these "preliminary" behaviors are not explicitly qualified by Freud as aesthetic, and if he does not evoke what is called an "art of loving,"[27] the fact remains that he explicitly derives the idea or sense of the beautiful from sexual attraction, and that he assigns a "sublimation" of sexual activity to artistic activity.[28] Whatever one might think of these schemas of derivation and sublimation (which are certainly questionable or at least capable of being interpreted in other terms), we must still agree that pleasure/displeasure is indeed the common denominator of all aisthetic activities considered in themselves and not for their different uses. In order to characterize this communal aisthetic, Freud gives a few indications that converge around what he designates by *rhythm*, as much around sex as around art—across these texts, a mutual echo can be observed between the rhythmics of the caress (which determine the possibility of singling out an "erotic zone") and the rhythmic model of poetry, whose implications we ought to extend across all

artistic fields. Rhythm—whose double value of scansion and schema (*ruthmos* initially had a meaning close to "figure") could no doubt be brought together to express a *pulse of nascent form* [*une* pulsation de la forme naissante]—should find its place in the analysis of drawing.

3. In this chiasmus of sensual and artistic aesthetics, the third conclusion therefore must establish that something is being played out that should not be reduced either to a sensualizing of art (as Freud rather believes, even though we cannot fully impute this to him), or to a simple aestheticization of eros. Even if it is legitimate to invoke the *ars amatoria* in all their possible forms, the work's irreducible difference nevertheless remains, as we have suggested. If sexuality is at work here, it is outside itself, in the child, which, moreover, is not exactly a work, because in the work the art or eros of its formation never ceases playing itself out, without giving place to another autonomous formation.

Distinct from these assimilations, a thought of form emerges according to the two directions of mobility (attraction, passage, progression, rhythmic beat) and determination (the election of a sensible field or register, of a zone or support—of a *medium*, as is said so inconsistently, since in art more than anywhere else, the *medium* is the "message," except that there is no message but an address or a touch). More basically, one could also say: the coupling of the forming form-force and the formed force-form [*la form/c/e formatrice et da la form/c/me formée*].

Without pressing further into Freud's thinking, suffice it to remark: in spite of himself, as it were—or rather, thanks to the uncertainties and reserves acknowledged in his text—Freud reveals in full a motif of form and its pleasure considered in themselves and existing in themselves once their presumed end (relaxation, entropy) also represents their overcoming. In fact, one could say that *art* appears as such only insofar as that pulsional goal [*destination pulsionnelle*] is not taken into account. But this also means that the moment of tension (and not intention!) in—and *as*—art is privileged, the moment of formative force more than that of the formed work, and that of pleasure desiring more than that of pleasure satisfied.

Keeping Freud's categories for a moment, one would be justified in saying that the pleasure of art is *perverse*, just as is, ultimately, all sexuality diverted from genital orgasm (whether leading to procreation or not, without entering here into a more nuanced examination of the problem).[29] In fact, one can always affirm that "art" properly understood (this belated and invariably controversial concept) is always the perversion of behaviors diverted from their cognitive, moral, religious, or political finalities. But this diversion is also what restrains all these finalities and all their satisfactions from representing themselves as possible, desirable, and consistent. (Is it not permissible to say that religious art protects religion from its fanatical drive?)

The *design* of art is its *idea* as idea—form, scheme, and rhythm—of that which is not achieved in any Idea, ideal, ideology, or ideation. It is the idea of that which repeatedly makes demands [*redemande*] on its own birth and the opening of its desire—drawing, intention to become enamored with oneself [*dessein de s'éprendre de soi*].

Sketchbook 9

"This discovery almost literally gave wings to the artist's hand. Not content simply to trace the shape of objects, this hand, enamored of its own movement and of that alone, described the involuntary figures within which, as experience has shown, these shapes were destined to become re-embodied . . . without preconceived intention, the pen that flows in order to write and the pencil that runs in order to draw out an infinitely precious substance, which, even if not always possessing an exchange value, nonetheless appears charged with all the emotional intensity stored up within the poet or painter at a given moment."

—André Breton, "Artistic Genesis and
Perspective of Surrealism"

"Above all, beauty pleases—it attracts the soul, which ugliness repels. Beauty is the pleasure of an attraction and the desire for this attraction itself."

—Plotinus, *First Ennead*

"Nietzsche thinks that without an overheated sexual system, Raphael would not have painted this crowd of Madonnas . . . this opinion leads to a sounder interpretation of pictorial phenomena."

—René Magritte, *Words and Images*

"Raphael and the others were men in whom the sensation was formulated before thought, which allowed them when studying never to destroy the sensation and to remain artists."

—Paul Gauguin, Letter to Émile Schuffenecker

"The artist is the hand which, through the proper use of touch (= form), creates vibrations in the human soul. It is therefore evident that the harmony of forms must rely only on the principle of entering into true contact with the human soul."

—Wassily Kandinsky, *On the Spiritual in Art*

"Pleasure would be a poor enough thing without this aberrant transcendency, not confined to sexual ecstasy and experienced in the same way by mystics of various religions, the Christian religion foremost. We receive being in an intolerable transcendence of being . . . and excess designates attraction [*l'attrait*]—the attraction if not horror of everything that is *more than is*."

—Georges Bataille, *Eroticism*

The Drawing/Design of the Arts

Allow me to add here a brief remark that will expand on several scattered notes in the previous pages concerning the plurality of the arts. What Freud has allowed us to designate as a counterpoint played out, according to a sexual score [*partition*], between different registers—"stages," "senses," and "zones"—ends up as playing a type of fugue or canon between artistic fields. In their relations of simultaneity and succession, of correspondence and distinction, in their mutual references and metaphors, or in the metonymy which makes them all express "art" (this singularity that is so difficult to decipher), the arts act simultaneously like stages, senses, and zones. Moreover, they also act as if attached to an infancy that never leaves them and that makes their story the history of an interminable repetition of their own birth (of the formation of their forms). And this birth is man's birth.

When he notes the impossibility, since this art still touches us, of reducing the art of the Greeks to their mythology, Marx writes: "A man cannot become a child again, or he becomes childish. But does he not find joy in the child's naïvité, and must he himself not strive to reproduce its truth at a higher stage?"[30] What makes truth and gives delight [*réjouissance*] out of naïveté is not ignorance but the emerging, innate (naive) character; it is the impetus of a form that that seeks itself and only finds itself in search of itself. Art shares the goal of playing out again an infancy of the senses and of sense (yet another singularity that is difficult to decipher), in other words, an infancy of our entire relation to the world. This playing out can be happy or painful. It can replay either the discovery of the world or the loss of the unreal outside of the world. It can either open or hollow out, or do both at once. This is always the effect of the way the mark, the tracing out, or the incision is drawn, dividing up areas, penetrating as well into the thickness that supports it.

The difference that Freud's sexual schema makes flagrant is in the way that the arts function as so many "perversions," which remain fixated at a stage, sense, or zone, and which are diverted from a final "relaxation." But this way of "remaining fixated"—whether to the visible, sonorous, or beating, or again, whether to the line, shading, and so on—is nowhere fixed in place. It is the choice of a momentary period during which stopping works to cultivate the intensity specific to a sensible difference, to differentiate it further, to bring out the specific drawing/design, and each time to extend and modulate a distinctive *mark* [trait], which will then be called, for better or worse, "painting" or "sculpture," "music" or "cinema."

In effect, art cannot be thought of as accomplishment—whether as the work's plenitude without remainder, as a common assumption in a "total art," or as the discharge of its energy for the benefit of some kind of engendering (of knowledge, belief, morality, civic-mindedness, etc.). But a second difference concerning art is that each of these "perversions"—which remain in a certain way closed in on themselves (painting does not become music, music does not become dance, etc., even if a common *drawing/design* traverses them)—aims at the same time to communicate itself and has a tendency to communicate its emotion to all others.

However, once the ambiguities tied to the motif of perversion have been raised (and thanks to the precautions that Freud himself takes in using the term, recalled earlier), one should not forget that art can be caught in a real perversion of its destination. We have learned at our expense—at the expense of our thought, our culture, and in certain respects, of art itself—what an absolutization of art, or worse, a "religion" or "metaphysics" of art can represent. Perhaps art is only itself when it appears as less of itself, when the aesthetic is displaced from all aestheticism, or when the desire for sensibility, or the pleasure of this desire, does not subject itself to any aesthetic, when it takes this pleasure secretly [*à la dérobée*],[31] in the margins of a celebratory, illustrative, or interpretive function, even of a possible "artistic" function, in this margin where a drawing silently displaces itself from the very design that commands it—which it has done, no doubt, right from the first traces of fingers or stone chisels guided by certain magical concerns. Art is no doubt foreign to "Art," to this artistic Art perceived as finery or temple, as bearer of messages or gratuitous exercise. "Art" is always a perversion of art.

In its own way, art remains inapparent [*inapparent*], and it is not the coming into appearance [*paraître*] or phenomenality that presents it—in short, one must be sensitive not just to the form but to the withdrawn movement of a formation. Being sensitive to it is not necessarily to be a "connoisseur" (a word that usually belongs to the artistic scene) but in effect to love, therefore to share this movement of form that desires itself, that desires its sense.

What Kant meant in speaking of aesthetic judgment's "claim to universality" suggests that art is devoted to the communication of sensibility, or more exactly, a sensibility communicating itself for itself, for its value or for its own *sense*, and not for its sensory, informational values—that is, for what we have called here *sensuality*. Art is communicated sensuality.[32] It desires to communicate itself to everyone, and the fact that only a few experience it does not invalidate it—it is not a question of social justice (even it is also a question of this) but something of the new form communicates itself from a few to many, perhaps to everyone. Art informs, deforms, and transforms a broad ensemble of forms around it, forms of objects but also forms of customs and forms of thought. Above all, it spreads imperceptibly something of its desire, of the new sensibility and sensuality for which it is the drawing/design.

Sketchbook 10

"The first sketches on the walls of caves set forth the world as 'to be painted' or 'to be sketched' and called for an indefinite future of painting, so that they speak to us and we answer them by metamorphoses in which they collaborate with us."

—Maurice Merleau-Ponty, *Signs*

"Many years later, one day studying the unfolding of lemmata neighboring Weierstrass's theorem, which states the notion of point and of the before and after on a straight line, I was suddenly overwhelmed by a sort of objectless exaltation, where there was joy, sadness, and suddenly I saw myself, lying on a bench, face on a folded jacket, trying to sleep but not sleeping. The obsession with the shared point of divide [*point de partage*] between two spaces, two influxes, had marked me from childhood and still does. And certainly, because it is more a mythical than terrestrial space, at the articulation of transcendence."

—Yves Bonnefoy, *The Hinterland*

"At the point of my brush, it happens—I live for moments like this—that I invent a mark [*trait*]. Sweetness, sharing: to recognize a mark!"

Pierre Alechinsky, *Excerpts on the (Por)trait*

"Line drawing emits its own light, created and not imitated."

—Pablo Picasso, *Writings on Art*

"All aesthetic form is a specific displacement through which form contradicts the identity it declares."

—Jacques Rancière, "Form and Its Spirit"

Mimesis

There are two fundamental attitudes toward *mimesis*, in other words, toward this notion for which we retain the Greek word in order to avoid any confusion with imitation, with simple and (as one often says) "servile" imitation. Indeed, the distinction between servility and mastery constitutes the axis that separates the two attitudes: either mimesis is subordinate to a model, or it dictates its law to it. From this, one can immediately draw a starker opposition between an imitation doomed to remain a vain reproduction and an enhancement whose inventiveness lessens the importance of the model in favor of that of the image. We know this contrast very well—the same contrast, for example, distinguishes an identity photo from a photographic portrait.

Mimetic ambivalence has played a decisive role in many episodes in the history of art. If art, in whatever form, is conceived as "representation," as staging, exhibition, or monstration of what is, the question arises of knowing

what is this "is," and how to show and (re)produce it—
how to draw it beyond a self-enclosed immediacy. Thus,
what "beautiful" form (of man, sentiment, thought) should
be elected if "beauty" must be found in that which renders
the being in question most manifest and desirable? (Plato
defines beauty as *ekphanestaton* and *erasmiōtaton* in the
Phaedrus [205d]—that which shines forth and is the most
desirable.)

The "being" in question is not given. To seek its form
and/or its beauty is precisely to seek its self ("man," "love,"
or "courage," "nature" or "movement," etc.). Whether
"imitative" or "representative," "realist" or "abstract," mimetic art is the technique that exposes what the given, as
given, does not make manifest—its very donation, its coming into view or into the world, the birth to form and thus,
identically, the form of its birth.

One can rightly be tempted to differentiate mimetic art
from an art that one calls "symbolic," an art presented to
us by African and Oceanic cultures. This would be an art
of forms given as signs ordering the world and not the
coming into the world. It is not the place here to pursue
the analysis of this distinction. Suffice it to remark that in
each regime there is something of the other, and that the
mimesis of the beautiful (true, good) form has a propensity
to join with the tracing out [*tracé*] of the sacred sign, with
the exception that its form is no longer received from a rite
and from its transmission, but must be found, invented,
and created. For the same reason, what is called here the
"sacred" is no longer constituted in any fashion; losing its
name in the process, it becomes, on the contrary, that

toward which a desire strives, which is the desire not of an object but of sense.

Mimesis gives rise to ambivalence, because the non-given must be sought through the given (the perceived, received, supple form), whereas for symbolic art there seem to be two distinct givens—sacred forms and profane forms. Thus, the idea of a simple conformity (however informed) to a "natural" given—the "true copy" [*copie conforme*]—is only possible through mistaking the being or truth in question. It is in this way that "servile" imitation is opposed to artistic "creation," or more exactly, it is in this way that the truth of art has repeatedly had to define itself against the conformity of the given. It has never ceased doing this, even at the height of the reign of "representation." Artistic form conforms only to the *artistic* truth toward which it gravitates and which directs its desire on each occasion. As Philippe Lacoue-Labarthe has repeated and articulated throughout all his work, the true character of mimesis is to be *without model*.

This truth is no less a *truth* and remains within the order of *knowledge*. It is knowledge that concerns us in mimesis, more exactly, knowledge as *pleasure*. That knowledge in general proceeds from pleasure, or rather, that we only seek to know because we desire pleasure [*jouir*], as Rousseau says, is the only hypothesis capable of explaining the quest for knowledge. Kant states (no doubt recalling Rousseau) that pleasure must be postulated at the origin of knowledge. It is perhaps through *mimesis* that this pleasure of knowing is illuminated.

Aristotle notes that men take pleasure in mimesis owing to the *mathesis* (of knowledge) that is obtained—in effect, mimesis is the instrument of recognition and identification. In front of representation, we say: "that's him, or her, or that!" As the *Poetics* states, this joyous surprise (of recognition) concludes a syllogism that should be understood not in the sense of the preestablished modes of a certain, probable, or invalid conclusion but in the wider sense of "reasoning," more exactly, from the relation or conjunction according to the *logos* or between *logoi* (reasons, judgments)—I conjoin the thing and the image according to the correspondence between a reality and its own form. If mimesis is a tendency before being a pleasure, or rather, if its pleasure comes from the satisfaction of a spontaneous tendency (here one should recall the numerous stories that attribute a pronounced and sometimes excessive penchant for drawing to young artists . . .), it is because man desires to give himself an identity as such, or the ownership [*propriété*] of the thing. What preoccupies him is not only the thing as the correlate of a need, appetite, or repulsion but the thing as "some-thing" and as the desirable and pleasurable propriety [*la propriété désirable et jouissive*] of this thing.

At the beginning of his "Remarks on 'Oedipus,'" Hölderlin writes: "Among mankind, one has to make sure with every thing that it is Something, i.e., that it is recognizable in the *medium (moyen) of its* appearance, that the way in which it is delimited can be determined and thought."[33]

This phrase condenses, transposes, even diverts [*détourne*] the Kantian notion of the "phenomenon" (of appearance). Instead of delimiting the field of legitimate knowledge as Kant does, Hölderlin states that the thing is above all what man can (or what he desires to) designate as "a thing," "this thing" (in its "manner of being"), and for this reason it stems from knowledge and not solely from an apprehension that conforms to a need. One could transcribe it as such: man's primary "need" (a desire, in truth, and not a need) is to know, in other words, to relate to the thing for itself, not simply to use (or consume) it. Because it is a desire, it is also a pleasure. It is the pleasure of desiring this relationship to the thing itself.

"Some-thing" is an isolated existence designated for its self. This *for itself* [pour soi] is its property, its distinctive character. The distinction does not apply simply between things (as the correlate between appetites, interests, etc.), but between the thing and its *being* as such. The *as* or the *as such* relates [*rapporte*] the thing to its self. It thus distinguishes its self in light of this relation. *Sameness* is not an essential identity replicated, which would, after all, only give rise to two identical things, two copies of the same thing. The *sameness* of the *very* thing [*la* mêmeté *de la chose* même] demands the relation of the thing to its own character, to its difference and its form, less in the sense of its fixed contour than in the sense of its formative principle.

A drawing shows us such a formative principle, or else the formation of (the form of) the thing. Drawing (including color, as needed[34]) responds to a mimetic tendency, which engenders the *mathesis* of the form—"it's him, her, that!" This knowledge gives pleasure, or better yet, it is pleasurable because its gives us a relation or because it lets us enter into a relation. It is the relation of sameness or of property. A dress drawn by Watteau is not only an example of fashion that may be used by costume designers. It is what is specific [*propre*] to the fabric, the drape, the envelopment and suggestion of the body, this specificity that, in order to take form, has been appropriated by a subject (mind, thought, talent, genius, sensibility).

In a much wider sense than is usually indicated by the term, whether in visual or written form, in general drawing/design (*dess[e]in* in both senses) constitutes a way of placing itself in contact with the formation of the form (of the thing, the thought, the emotion . . .). It is opened up by seeking the way it coincides with the most profound and secret movement of an appearance [*apparaître*] or a coming into appearance [*paraître*]—how is it *specifically*? How *exactly* does it form itself? What is its particular energy? What is its force and how does it come into being? How is it formed? Little by little, what is at stake each time is nothing less than: how does the world form itself and how am I allowed to embrace its movement? *Mimesis* proceeds from the desire of *methexis*—of participation—in what plays out before the birth of the world; in its profound truth, *mimesis* desires to imitate the inimitable "creation," or more simply, the inimitable and unimaginable uprising [*surgissement*] of being in general.

Sketchbook 11

"His line is so narrow, still so surrounded by large fields of emptiness. And in consequence so easy for him to sense [*pressentir*] that this white page is the non-knowledge that overflows his ability to know."

—Yves Bonnefoy, *The Wandering Life*

"Figurative or not, the line is no longer a thing or an imitation of a thing. It is a certain disequilibrium kept up within the indifference of the white paper; it is a certain process of gouging within the in-itself, a certain constitutive emptiness. . . . The line is no longer the apparition of an entity upon a vacant background, as it was in classical geometry. It is, as in modern geometries, the restriction, segregation, or modulation of a pre-given spatiality."

—Maurice Merleau-Ponty, *Eye and Mind*

"When the sun is most beautiful, I go out in the morning. I make a sketch near to the stone bridge, of the river fleeing in the distance, a picturesque bouquet of trees in the foreground. I walk about happily."

—Eugène Delacroix, *Journal*

"His mark [*trait*] does not establish a scene that he already has in mind, which could be described in imagination as whatever being happens to pass before his eyes. What he traces is nothing other than he himself who takes this impetus and leaps up without anything. And what is he other than this fortuitous mark?"

—Max Loreau, *Of Creation*

Pleasure of Relation

If this is the case, and if there is pleasure there, it is because pleasure in general is tied to a relation, to the perception of a relation or to its enactment, two possibilities that, no doubt, intersect or even come together. Pleasure is in the relation that tends toward its prolongation or its repetition, just as displeasure tends toward suspending and rejecting the relation. One finds pleasure or displeasure *at* [à] such and such a form, such and such an encounter—that thing or event *makes* or *creates* pleasure for us, we *take* pleasure in it. Pleasure is indissociable from this active and passive tension, from this receptive spontaneity.

To know (*sapere*) is first of all to have taste, in both senses of the expression—to isolate a particular flavor or to be truly capable of appreciating it. *Homo sapiens* is the animal gifted with a taste for the unique savoring of things, for savoring the world as world, in other words, as the coming into appearance, release, and compearance [*paraître, parution et comparution*] of all things together and in their indefinite multiplicity.[35] It is the animal that has a taste for this compearance as such, as the relation to itself of being in its givenness [*rapport à soi de l'être-donné*], which also means, as the gift of this donation. The gift, the formation of all forms, in other words, of all presences, is world's relation to itself.

We should specify what *relation* is in general. Relation distinguishes itself from being, insofar as one understands "being" following the example of common tradition and grammar as an intransitive verb. (We won't explore this further, but it is Heidegger who asks that we understand being as transitive, as if *to be* and *to make* or *to take* had the same syntax.) Relation is not exactly transitive—it is transitivity, transit, transport. It is the effect [*l'efficace*] of one subject toward another, with its reciprocal necessity, and it thus involves the transport between them of some thing, force, or form that affects them both [*l'un de l'autre*] and modifies—or at least modalizes—them both [*l'un par l'autre*]. Relation suggests modification, modalization, and modulation, rather than substance, instance, or essence. Relation suggests, if not transformation in the fullest sense of the term, at least the displacement, movement, or alteration of form.

Relation affects a subject. This is how the subject becomes subject and not substance. What one calls "subject" is a relational force [*puissance*], as much active as passive, an ability to affect and be affected—the force from the outside, or more precisely, the force of sharing and opening between an *inside* and *outside* which refer to one another. It is through this that the subject *relates itself* to its self [se rapporte *à soi*], in other words, distinguishes itself from its self and experiences itself as distinct—the other in its self, experiencing this alterity as its own, experiencing its self as other. Relation is an alterity or alteration that does not happen to the subject by accident but is essential to it. To be sure, sexual pleasure should also be first considered in this perspective, or rather, it ought to be.[36]

Divided up into *inside/outside*, *same/other*, and *one/two*, the subject either puts further demands on itself [*se redemande*] according to these divisions, or it rejects itself. Pleasure lies in the revival of alteration (in fact, indefinitely); displeasure lies in its rejection.

One understands this better if one considers again that pleasure defined as such must be distinguished from the pleasure of satisfaction through which a need is satisfied. Plato understands this well—the suspension of a lack is only a form of pleasure, which should not be confused with the pleasure of desiring. The pleasure of quenching one's thirst differs from the pleasure of tasting a delectable drink—in the first case, a tension is overcome, while in the second a tension is preserved and promises to return. The first case plays out in a finite completion (one is no longer thirsty), the second in an infinitude that thwarts both completion and incompletion together. This infinitude is the movement of a revived relation (inside/outside, same/other, one/two). More rigorously, one should say that *pleasure*, if one maintains its value of attraction and revived intensity (its value of self-desire), ought to be distinguished from "satisfaction" or "contentment." What satisfies is a thing (an object, a being), what gives pleasure is a relation (an opening, an alteration). My pleasure relates me in my-self [*me rapporte en moi*] to a subject that "I" am not, which is prior to and beyond me, to my desire and my pulsion [*pulsion*].

In antiquity, pleasure is dependent on the perception or sharing of *harmony* or fit [*convenance*]—in other words, on what provides a model of relation. But even outside this classical perspective, the relation that tends toward pre-serving itself or to its own growth—the relation that re-vives itself or that (in Valéry's term) *puts further demands on itself* [se redemande]—is always *a coming together* [con-venance] or "harmony." If it is not harmonic in the sense of a regularity, it is in the sense of an articulation, of some form of adjoining (a motif that recalls the Greek sense of *harmonia*). "That suits me" is an extremely banal phrase, at once subjective and relative. But the same phrase can take on another tone—thus, I can accept a challenge whose magnitude I cannot measure, to which I give myself with-out measure. No doubt, such is always the initial access to a work of art.

The very fact that regularity in any tradition is either posited or sought, diverted or complicated to the point of losing regularity (or no longer associated with a law, norm, or rule) indicates that it is only ever present as a line of flight and as the hyperbole of good fit [*convenance*] in gen-eral. This presence does not imply an external conform-ity but an assemblage [*agencement*] of parts (segments, moments, aspects) that do not necessarily obey a pre-established schema (pre-drawn, schematized) but which mutually confer their coming together [*con-venance*], the possibility for them to join together, to form an articulation or correspondence, to respond to one another, to refer to one another, to con-figure themselves. This is called *rhythm*, which in Greek is initially a configuration—quite simply, the fact of not escaping into infinity but of coming back toward one's self and of turning the division of space, the cut which opens it, into a curve that folds it without closing it. In the same way, the succession of equal times can be scanned in a beat, curving time onto itself in *measures* [temps] that respond to themselves and draw the possibility of a line that one calls melodic.

Ultimately, mimesis is nothing other than a rhythmics of appearance through which the mystery—or the evidence—of the rising or suspension [*la levée*] of forms in general is known, is recognized, and participates. In all its possible forms—a line traced by a pencil, by a dancer, a voice, or an editing console—drawing/design must be understood as engaging a rhythm, setting in play a beat, a differentiation, displacements, folds, and connections of the indistinct, of what is simply always itself [*simplement-égal-a-soi*]. The architect Henri Gaudin once remarked: "In drawing, space begins to vibrate, systole and diastole; my thirst for the world breaks the line, I erase, I cross out . . ." What is called "the happy mark [*le trait heureux*]" owes its happiness—its *bon heur*, its good fortune—to this rupture of given forms, to this unguided pursuit of what gives of itself as true vibration. This truth is not attested by any conformity but always by the rising/suspension [*la levée*] of a line in accord with its impetus alone.

Sketchbook 12

"Situate the *beautiful* in the perception of relations and you will have the story of its progress from the birth of the world up to today. Choose the differential character of the beautiful in general, another such quality that will please you, and your idea will be suddenly concentrated in a point in space and time."

—Denis Diderot, "Philosophical Research on the Origin and Nature of the Beautiful"

"These parts [of music] are constrained to arise and to die in one or more harmonic tempos which surround a proportionality by its members; such a harmony is composed not differently from the circumferential line which generates human beauty by its [respective] members."

—Leonardo da Vinci, *Treatise on Painting*

"The line, . . . uprising [*surgissement*], a gust that flows back in order to gush again, an uninterrupted propulsion against the constructed form, that which produces it carries it to the end without letting it disintegrate. Its achievement does not assume an end but, on the contrary, a slit—the largest naturally rectilinear and un-innocent rip, the kind that allows one to catch a glimpse of the secret attachment between two things and therefore the relations that had been unperceived until then, the initial identity of the real before the word that we call poetry."

—René Char, "Search for the Base and the Summit"

"Each drawing abounds in, liberates an ensemble of correspondences, a network of equivalences, triggering exchanges between the inanimate and the living, the near and the far, the miniscule and the immense."

—Luc Richir, "Drawing"

"Through the magic of the line [*trait*], what makes the simple contrast between black and white come into appearance is this presence of the extraordinary in the ordinary, that alone grants to man a sojourn."

—Francoise Dastur, *At the Birth of Things*

"The representation of pleasure is itself amusing [*plaisante*]. What is specific to love [*la propriété de l'amour*] is to take pleasure in [*jouir*] the idea of a being that we represent to ourselves, imagining that he makes us come. And so the lovers dream of his pleasure, because that itself gives him pleasure."

—François Zourabichvili, *Spinoza:
A Physics of Thought*

Death, Sex, Love of the Invisible

If pleasure stems from the relation of the thing to itself—as itself, and as this "its self" is not given once and for all, nor conforms to any use of the thing—then this pleasure is always a new version of the relation of the thing to its own appearance and disappearance. In effect, whether this "thing" consists in the representation of an object or a body from the perceived world, or whether it remains in a form without reference, what matters in it is the movement that detaches it from the formless [*informe*] in whose ground [*au fond*] nothing is distinguished. Drawing draws its mark [*trait*] from this withdrawing [*retrait*], and throughout the time it maintains its mark, throughout the formation of its form, it does so in an extended, imminent, trembling, and menacing relation—with this chaotic and viscous obscurity whence all form emanates and to which it returns.

The place that is estranged from all forms—a place, therefore, that is itself outside all place, a place without localization or consistence—is indicated in a special manner by two representations that act as representations of the unrepresentable—that of death, and that of sex. These are not allegorical representations of the abstractions "death" and "sex" but representations of a dead person—a cadaver—and of the organs of sexual reproduction. It is not by chance that these two kinds of representation are found posited at the beginning and end of the history of mimesis—Aristotle at the beginning, Freud at the end.

After having shown that we take pleasure in representations because they teach us how to recognize things—"that's it!" we say—Aristotle adds that we take pleasure in the representation of things that, in reality, repulse us, things like cadavers or hideous animals in particular. Having outlined the trajectory from "fore-pleasure" to "terminal pleasure," Freud adds in a note that the origin of the sense of beauty is found in this sexual seduction and that "the fact that genital organs themselves are not considered beautiful must be put in relation to this fact [of the origin of the beautiful in sexuality]." This interaction must consist clearly in understanding that access to what in itself cannot be beautiful demands the mediation of seduction, in other words, of "fore-pleasure." It is the same for access to sex properly understood as it is for gaining access to the cadaver or the repulsive in general—the play of forms renders bearable the formlessness of dead flesh and obscene flesh equally. In effect, they are both presented at the limit of blurring and, ultimately, in a disappearance of forms, whose common element could be characterized by the diverse stages or states of viscosity, stickiness, sliminess, and humidity in general, insofar as they are not resolved into clarity and liquid purity.

Freud's affirmation is both confirmed and invalidated by the testimony of artists. On the one hand, Leonardo da Vinci notes: "The act of copulation and the members employed are so repulsive, that if it were not for the beauty of faces and the adornments of the actors and unbridled passion, nature would lose the human species."[37] On the other, William Blake writes in "The Marriage of Heaven and Hell": "The soul of sweet delight can never be defiled. . . . The head Sublime, the heart Pathos, the genitals Beauty, the hands and feet Proportion. . . . Exuberance is Beauty . . . . Enough! or Too much!"[38]

At the same time, we can see that Blake's affirmation is doubly posed, as an exigency or protestation raised against the inverse affirmation, which is implicitly that of common sense (or common morality). Blake is interested in, on the one hand, rejecting a possible "defiling" of pleasure, and on the other, in affirming an excess ("exuberance," "too much") constitutive of beauty.

The same excess is found in Aristotle and Freud, without either of them recognizing it as such. The practice of forms only applies insofar as it is extended toward something like an excess or exuberance, an expansion that cannot know its limit a priori because it must always be in order to begin and (in reproduction and death) finish with a relation to the excess of form [*l'outre-forme*]. In such a relation, on the one hand, one could say that the form tames the formless and makes it visible, but, on the other hand it does not do so without touching its own limit, and thus opening onto the invisible itself.

Aristotelian recognition—the "that's it!" whose exclamation expresses pleasure—has as a tendency and an ultimate tension the recognition of this double limit of origin and end. "That's it—the very thing that escapes all identification! Here's the origin and end!" In a certain way, this exclamation of art in general, and more precisely, of what drawing in its most expansive sense comes to trace (a line, a gesture, a visual, sonorous, or tactile impetus . . .) is what drawing comes to open and does not close off, that for which it is sensibly and sensually the exclamation. Drawing identifies what precedes and follows identity, what escapes far away from it toward virgin or saturated spaces, but in any event without forms from beyond all our possible worlds.

Extending Aristotle and Freud in a certain way, one might still add that the function of art is not different from that of love—beyond representation, the cadaver remains beautiful for the mourner who gazes at it with love, and sexual organs are beautiful for lovers without art having to render them decent.[39] But what love does for two, art does for an entire community.

And yet artistic practices proceed from a form of love— the love of forms, understood not as taste for beautiful forms (since the notions of "taste" and the "beautiful" can only come after the movement of this love and the creative desire of forms) but as gesture extended toward the formation of forms, as creative genius of forms (as one used to say long ago), which alone enables the opening of the world to the truth of its origin and end—in other words, to the appearance/disappearance of being "for the beauty of its gesture." That the beauty of this gesture has been represented as a divine gesture nowhere folds art back onto religion—on the contrary. It makes art something like an adoration whose gestural pleasure would be prayer—liberated from all worship and all pious comfort (including that of aestheticizing devotions).

The legendary stories told repeatedly of artists in their childhood testifies to the fervor of this gesture. Curiously, in the case of drawing, and even if music gives rise to similar stories, there exists a cliché of the future artist seized right from birth by the fever of drawing. In the Preface to *Lives of the Painters*, Vasari declares: "And if in our own times it has been seen (as I trust to be able to demonstrate a little later by many examples) that simple children roughly reared in the woods, with their only model in the beautiful pictures and sculptures of nature, and by the vivacity of their wit, have begun by themselves to make designs."[40]

Across the *Lives* that follow, examples of this are numerous, the most celebrated being that of Michelangelo, whom we cited earlier, as well as several others. The origin of this topos appears to be found in a story about Giotto, which Vasari reconstructs in these terms:

When he had come to the age of ten, he showed in all his actions, although childish still, a vivacity and readiness of intelligence much out of the ordinary, which rendered him dear not only to his father but to all those also who knew him, both in the village and beyond. Now Bondone gave some sheep into his charge, and he, going about the holding, now in one part and now in another, to graze them, and impelled by a natural inclination to the art of design, was for ever drawing, on stones, on the ground, or on sand, something from nature, or in truth anything that came into his fancy.[41]

Just as the story and/or the legend about Giotto fulfills an exemplary function for the lives of the painters, so this general legend of drawing (which, of course, must be aligned with the true taste for drawing that young children very often show) plays an exemplary role for art in general. Drawing calls for the representation of an innate disposition, a spontaneous taste and pleasure, a desire that seizes the mind and guides the hand.

Of course, this legend also tends to cover over all the work necessary for the exercise of art, all the discipline, constraints, and pain, not only of the necessary work but also of the effort extended toward what the artist invariably knows will remain beyond the completed work. But this pain itself testifies to the renewed tension of a desire that makes demands on itself, inhabited by the desire to render sensible what can only escape from the senses just as much as from Sense taken absolutely—once again, the formless or the beyond-form of the origin-end.

The fever of drawing, the fever of art in general, is born of the frenzied desire to push form right to the limit, to make contact with the formless, as an erotic fever pushes bodies to the limits of their own forms.

Sketchbook 13

"Pure drawing is the material visibility of the invisible"
—Alain Badiou, "Drawing"

"The sight of a masterpiece stops you in spite of yourself, captivates you in a reverie to which nothing calls you except an invincible charm. This silent charm works with the same force and seems to increase every time you cast your eyes on it."

—Eugène Delacroix, *Journal*

"I live in a pleasant room with dark woodwork, outside the city, and the view from the window is so exquisite that I could not stop myself from drawing it."

—Robert Walser, *Life of the Poet*

"The will is necessary for seeing; and both the end and the means of this willed seeing is the drawing itself."

—Paul Valéry, *Degas, Dance, Drawing*

"What guides the graphic point, the quill, pencil, or scalpel, is the respectful observance of a commandment, the acknowledgment before knowledge, the gratitude of the receiving before seeing, the blessing before knowledge"

—Jacques Derrida, *Memoirs of the Blind*

". . . he followed his penchant, learnt to draw and paint, passing his life drawing everything that he encountered; Greuze said it well—he had a priapism of drawing."

—Charles-Germain de Saint-Aubin on his
brother Gabriel, cited by Pierre Rosenberg in
The Book of the Saint-Aubins

"The most unremarkable object that in itself would be totally incapable of arousing a feeling of pleasure in us can generate a very pleasant feeling when the imagination or a certain enthusiasm pushes us to find it beautiful."

—Johann Georg Sulzer, *A New Theory of Pleasures*

Ambiguous Pleasure

Signs of an ambiguity essential to pleasure have appeared on several occasions in the preceding pages, over and beyond the diversity of meanings that the word *pleasure* can convey. This ambiguity should be addressed directly.

Pleasure is either calming or stimulating. For Plato, there is pleasure through the suspension of pain, and there is pleasure through the increase of enjoyment. For Aristotle, the pleasure [*agrément*] of recognition and protective distance with respect to the hideous object go hand in hand. For Freud, lowering tension and form extended toward such a decrease should be associated. Derrida's reading of Freud emphasizes to what extent *Beyond the Pleasure Principle* does not conclude with any thesis (in the fullest sense of the word), insofar as this "beyond" is still suspected of returning to a type of pleasure (which, if it is the pleasure of death, can only be terrible for consciousness, but is pleasure nonetheless). We should recall that for Burke and Kant, as well as for any thinking of the sublime after them, the sublime sentiment carries a mixture of pleasure and displeasure, as well as a contagion of form by the formless. Finally, we have seen how a relation threatened at its origin and end by formlessness seems to delineate quite clearly the extremities of all thought concerning forms.

Ambiguity thus seems to be constitutive of pleasure—if it pleases and if, in pleasing, it satisfies, it borders on displeasure. If it stimulates, its very excitation, its tension is displeasurable. To understand this, we must recognize two conditions: (1) satisfaction is not mere relaxation, and (2) displeasure is not mere pain.

Between them, the two conditions are tangential and intersect [*sécantes*]. They point toward a third area—a regime that cannot be reduced either to the position of satisfaction or to that of pain. My hypothesis will be that this regime is specifically one of what we call "pleasure." Or again, the essence of pleasure cannot be reduced to a simple positivity. Pleasure is not simple or single . . .

Stated as necessary conditions of the ambiguity of pleasure, one must first unfold the content of these two propositions:

1. Satisfaction is not mere relaxation. This affirmation can be understood if one considers that mere relaxation, the state of accomplished entropy, presupposes the return of the tensioning (and tensioned) apparatus to a state in which tension is excluded and thus not even presented as virtual (if *virtuality* signifies nothing other than *potentiality*, power [*puissance*] understood in the sense of both reserve and force). The state that is properly relaxed is not a tension in reserve—in short, it is the inorganic or death, considered as pure immanence or an identity without a

relation to itself. If such a state is called "satisfaction," then we understand that this word must be understood in the fullest sense as *satis* ("enough, in complete sufficiency") and in the most complete sense of the *factum* ("made, finished, terminated"). Thus, the true meaning of the word will be "repletion." Repletion no longer knows pleasure. It shifts into satiety (the fulfilled *satis*); it falls into a sleep that does not renew emotion but stultifies and anesthetizes it. For pleasure demands a relation to the self—nothing gives me pleasure if I do not *please myself in taking pleasure in it*. It is no different for any other kind of sensing [*sentir*]— sensation and/or feeling. To feel signifies to feel oneself feeling, in other words, quite simply to relate to oneself the effect—and thus the affect—of a non-self or exteriority [*un dehors*] (whether "one's own body" or the supposed "subject" itself).

Under these conditions, the "discharge" achieved would liquidate the relation to the self or the subject, and thus it would not be experienced as release or relaxation. Conversely, if it is experienced (felt), it is still implicated in the tension of this "to itself." Besides, in reality there is never self-substance; there is only self as "to itself," in other words, aimed toward "self," which is not a specified goal but, as it were, the tension's extension. To conceive of a pleasure of relaxation is to conceive of a pleasure of death, as Freud did, following others.[42] This means to conceive of the subject experiencing itself in death, feeling itself dead, and rejoicing in its own absence of self—nothing less than the Hegelian Spirit understood not in a heroic mode alone but in delight at its heroism.

There can be no pure relaxation. Pleasure always demands the tension of self-affection or a feeling of self in which all being-itself finally consists—in other words, the possibility of distinguishing itself from an "outside" and of relating it to itself or of relating self to it. In another way, it is the possibility of *feeling*. Relaxation without remainder would be the unbinding of feeling. Inasmuch as there is "discharge," such an unbinding or loss of consciousness is indeed produced. However, pleasure experiencing itself still aims [*se tend*] beyond itself.

2. Displeasure is not mere pain. What pleasure wants insofar as it is desire of self is no doubt the suppression of exteriority, the resorption of the outside or of the non-self. But since pleasure must experience this resorption, it puts it at a distance. In distancing itself, it renews in itself a tension that affects it, and so becomes painful to itself. Here we reencounter Freud's quandary—how can a tension be pleasurable? Instead of replying, as does Freud, by citing the purposiveness of this tension, we would answer by pointing to the tension itself, or its *tonos*. Once again, here Eros and the Muses take on the same allure (taking into account the difference of the work): in accomplishment, it is not a conclusion that is played out but a pause, a breath taken in the rhythm of the *tonos*. For neither tension nor tone is without rhythm. To draw a line is not to make a mark—as we know, it is "to follow one's desire," and in order to do this, to feel desire announcing itself, taking shape, complicating itself, dividing itself, and so on.

Perhaps it is possible, then, to sketch out an approach to something that will undoubtedly remain difficult to understand, something that originates less from comprehension than sensible apprehension: there exists a displeasure that is not the opposite of pleasure or its adversary, but that comes from (dis)pleasure itself and from the impossibility—or rather, the undesirable character—of the resolution or dissolution of tensions that it seems at first to have promised. What pleasure demands proves to be fundamentally contradictory—it desires the suppression *and* the maintaining and even increase of tension. Thus, in the end, it cannot avoid deceiving itself, whether through a suppression that leaves it nothing else to experience, or through a maintaining or increase, which makes it experience a renewed distance from its own goal. In either case, pleasure (which desires itself) encounters the impossibility of fulfillment (in other words, of pleasing itself) without itself being affected by excess or lack.

This impossibility is inherent in pleasure's most intimate possibility—it is only possible in relation to a sense of powerlessness or of an excess of power. More exactly and more simply, pleasure consists in "making repeated demands on itself" [*un "se redemander soi même"*], which includes an essential inconsistency [*inconsistence*] in the "its self" in question here (or perhaps an essential *desistance*, to take up the term Derrida reworks from the writings of Lacoue-Labarthe).[43]

(Without taking it up further here, we should note in passing that this essential inconsistency or desistance—or again, what is called the subject's insubstantiality—immediately orients us toward the constitution or the very nature of the *subject* in general, and according to all its modalities. Pleasure—in other words, to restate this once again, desire of self [*le désir de soi*]—sets the tone for the subject or the fundamental register of the subject. It affects and extends itself, not strictly speaking "toward itself," since the "self" is not exactly given (whether as origin or end) but *in itself* [en soi]. "In itself" is desire of self; it affects itself [*il s'affecte lui-même*], which is to say that this "in itself" is not an interiority but the differentiation according to which an "inside" and "outside" can be represented, being the two faces of "self." One might say without objection: "its body" and "its soul," and one will understand by this that "all pleasure is bodily" (as Kant likes to repeat, following Epicurus). This signifies nothing more than that all pleasure aims toward the coming together [*convenance*] of an "outside" and an "inside" whose distinction and relation are opened by *feeling*. But this pleasure takes place only insofar as this coming together remains exposed as such, in other words, experienced and felt, not resolved in indistinction. The subject is distinction—between the self and others, but before all else, between self and self. The subject is an endless mark [*trait*] drawn from self to self, but never like a "drawn line" [*trait tiré*], since there are no rules. The subject is a mark stretched out at length from subject to subject, with detours, contours, divisions, and spirals. Here we have the attraction of this line [*l'attrait de ce trait*] and the perpetually renewed retraction from a conclusion: for in order to end, the mark effaces itself and carries off with it any figure outlined. If it effaces the figure, it also revives the sketch of its very effacement. A subject is a sketch, an outline, a draft—not the draft of a self continually (and desperately) to come, but the self extended, thrown, risked, exposed.)

The impossibility of and in pleasure's specific possibility obviously brings a displeasure that is immanent to pleasure—the sorrow [*peine*] of losing oneself, or the sorrow in finding oneself, the unpleasant character of the already past or the still elusive, two modalities in which the past and future combine together. Pleasure replays by itself the aporetic scene of the present moment—it is never there, it escapes itself in its own passing. It is in this way that it delights [*jouit*]; it is in this way that it struggles to be delighted; and it is in this way that it delights in its sorrow. It is never satisfied, always lacking a before and after, and yet finding pleasure from and in this very displacement. The same for one sex in another, by the other, and toward the other; "sex" means the pleasure and sorrow of relating oneself [*s'envoyer*] into the other.

Sorrow is the suitable term for this displeasure that comes to pleasure, because it is not pain or suffering, which both designate types of intrusion whose source does not lie in the desire specific to pleasure. No doubt pain and suffering can also stem from this desire, and they can accompany the sorrow to which we are referring here. But they themselves have another nature. *Sorrow* represents an affliction inflicted because of a lack; it is punishment, chastisement. Pleasure chastises itself at once for wanting to realize itself and for not being able to do so. There is nothing moral here, even if it is easy to understand how a moralizing of the punishment immanent in pleasure can be grafted onto its innermost economy. Nothing moral, then, but rather what might well be called an ethics of pleasure: a pleasure that does not let itself be satisfied, that refuses satiety, and whose exigency never fails to turn into sorrow.

The pleasure of art is only restful in relation to a relative stability of the work [*œuvre*]. But the work undoes itself by itself [*se défait d'elle même*]—it makes demands on itself; it reopens the desire from which it has arisen. It cannot be confounded with work [*ouvrage*]. All its force resides in what makes it sorrow over itself, its idea or form. In sorrow—lacking relief, suffering, in suspense, in desire for what it knows can only satisfy though repeated excitation.

(The artist's sorrow, suffering, weariness, and discouragement. Certainly there is a whole romantic pathos surrounding the pain of engendering art, inflected as if in response to traditional legends about the pleasures of young artists. But in spite of the complacent excess of this pathos, one cannot misrecognize the tension and thus the sorrow that the work demands—in other words, the harassing and inherently impossible calculation of an achievement without end, a completion without closure and totality.)

Sketchbook 14

"I nearly always have my drawing notebook in hand when walking the streets, so as to master little by little the movements of men and animals, which no professor can teach, and which is most important."

—August Macke, *Letter to his parents*

"That is the sense, so it seems to me, in which art may be said to imitate nature, namely, by the life that the creative worker infuses into the work of art. The work will then appear as fertile and as possessed of the same power to thrill, the same resplendent beauty as we find in works of nature.

Great love is needed to achieve this effect, a love capable of inspiring and sustaining that patient striving toward truth, that glowing warmth and that analytic profundity [*dépouillement profond*] that accompany the birth of any work of art. But is not love the origin of all creation?"

—Henri Matisse, *Writings on Art*

"Except for the difference in character, defined by interior tensions, and except for the process of formation, the origin of all lines is the same: force"

—Wassily Kandinsky, *Point and Line to Plane*

"Contrary to what one thinks, art demands above all that one make it or experience it, joy and sincerity, innocence and flexibility. Ruses and suffering come by themselves; there is no need to summon them."

—Jean-Christophe Bailly, *A Night in the Library*

"There are many people who have a desire for and love of drawing, but no aptitude for it, and this can be discerned in children if they are not diligent and never finish their copies with shading."

—Leonardo da Vinci, *Notebooks*

Purposiveness Without Purpose

The formula with which Kant characterizes the specificity of aesthetic judgment—that is to say, *purposiveness without purpose*—remains the matrix for all investigation into the subject of the beautiful or art. "Aesthetic judgment" here designates the judgment that declares *beautiful* a reality (thing or work) insofar as such a judgment is primarily considered not in its actual use but in its a priori possibility. It is not about the implications of my decision to declare, for example, such and such a film "beautiful," but of the general condition that allows me to speak of the "beauti-ful" (instead of saying only that "this film is pleasant, en-tertaining, interesting . . ."). This condition is thus immediately social or communal; to say "this is beautiful" implies addressing oneself to all (at least to a very large group, to an entire culture), while to say "this is pleasant to me" only concerns myself. The first judgment involves others, places me in relation to them, while the second, on the contrary, severs me off.

Essential to the aesthetic order, this condition of *address*, *relation*, and potential *sharing* [partage] is given in the concept of *purposiveness without purpose*. Its content is far from reducing itself to a more or less dialectical self-annulment, as in *X without X*. On the contrary, the *purposiveness* and the *purpose* do not overlap. The stakes consist precisely in thinking the former without the latter—we designate as beautiful what orients itself according to a direction, or even according to a destination to which no end can be assigned. By "end," we mean the culmination of the purposiveness, inasmuch as this culmination posits itself beyond a directional movement. The attained and realized end effaces the purposiveness within it. In order to find this purposiveness again, the *finite* aspect of and in the end must be displaced in its order and dissolved. Thus, once reached, the goal of a voyage (a town, a visit, a task) can change its appearance quite significantly if one attempts to find there the voyage itself—while it makes sense to tell the adventure of discovering Timbuktu, it no longer makes sense to recount the trip at the end of which I made a deal in Timbuktu to set up a business.

Purposiveness without purpose thus constitutes a purposiveness devoid of purpose, end, or conclusion that is nevertheless a *purposiveness*, the pursuit of a purpose, an end. However, this end cannot be properly designated or fixed. Purposiveness postpones or delays the end. It displaces it without end, meaning interminably. But this interminable pursuit forms the purposiveness, its tension, as it were, considered according to its extension and expansion rather than its intention.

This can be stated in a different way by designating this tension as *drawing*. In effect, as *designation* and showing [*monstration*] or also as *taikan* (another etymology from the Germanic language which relates to *Zeichung*, *drawing*, *dibujo*, and which also allegedly touches on *disegno*)— in other words, placing into evidence and discourse— drawing as designing of the true (just and/or beautiful) form represents the pursuit of this form, the pursuit of the truth of the thing becoming visible [*du paraître*], in other words, of the thing itself.[44] For this becoming visible is strictly irreducible to appearance, or to the being that has appeared, which, as such, no longer comes into view but is only given and posed as object. On the contrary, this becoming visible or coming into visibility [*le paraissant*] *is given*, and it only "is" in and as this *gift*. The being of the gift cannot be given, and in this sense it is not *being*. It makes or it lets exist all being without itself having anything of being.

To pursue the form of the becoming visible—the form coming into visibility and the becoming visible of form, *forma formans*—amounts to pursuing what is stripped bare [*se dérobe*] or withdraws in appearance while opening it and making it possible. This amounts to following the trace [*se mettre sur la trace*] of such a withdrawal [*retrait*], or rather of such a *withdrawing* [*retirement*]. Drawing wants to show the truth, not of what has appeared or its appearance but of the coming into appearance [*l'apparaître*] that subtends it and that "itself" does not appear or show itself. Thus, it is about showing what does not show itself. More precisely, it is not about showing *what* does not show itself (that would be contradictory), nor even showing *that* something does not show itself (that would be of the order of the concept, not of a coming into visibility, and, moreover, one cannot think of that as "something"). It is about showing the infinity of becoming visible; the movement through which appearance is possible cannot itself be finished, that appearance is necessarily *finite* (accomplished form, achieved contour detached on a ground). This does not signify that this movement continues indefinitely in the order of appearances (as if it were retracing them ceaselessly, and thus blurring or overloading them, which is sometimes what a draftsman does by design), but rather that it is infinite by nature, in the sense of an actual (and not potential) infinitude. The infinity of becoming visible is of the order of divisibility of a finite line into points—infinite divisibility, as one knows, and strict ("one-to-one") correspondence of infinite ensembles thus revealed in different length segments. Thus, what is expressed by division and enumeration of the logic is expressed in the register of gesture and physical participation (corporeal, emotional, responsive) in the tracing of the line. Just as all lines in all drawings include the same infinity of points, so together they all respond with the same, endlessly modulated gesture, opening to infinitude.

The line, or the mark, or better yet, the tracing of the line—this gesture is nothing other than the infinite in actuality that drawing shows us, that it extends toward us so that we produce it again within us, so that we ourselves become mimesis of this mimesis of the birth to form. This includes *methexis* as well—I embrace the line that I am gazing at or the musical movement that I hear. Their desire is reborn in me and for me—or rather, in a withdrawn body [*corps retiré*] that is not "me" but the other "self" in me that harmonizes with this motion and emotion.

How could we not understand drawing according to this ethics in which, no doubt, we shall find the initial ethics of everything we call art, or the originary ethics of aesthetics as exemplified, as it were, by drawing in its most extended form—a desire to be pleased by a thing that it is not limited to the completion of an appearance, a signification, or a destination? This is the desire, then, that the thing itself desires in its true form, in other words, a desire that is impossible to fulfill or bring to completion: a desire that is infinite and *unfinishable*—in short, a desire to appropriate the thing (whatever it might be—object or gesture, subject matter or size, scene or outline) in the movement of a pleasure through which the thing relates itself to it*self*, to the possibility that the thing affects to (and by) itself [*s'affecte (d')elle-même*].

One might also say that the thing relates itself to me, to the *self* of an "artist" or a "art lover," but it concerns a single process—that of rendering an event [*circonstance*] of the world (a volume, a displacement, a weight, a mixture, an inflection, etc.) to its pure, originary possibility, to an uprising [*surgissement*] that owes nothing more to any use or perception than its coming, its sudden arising [*survenue*], which does nothing but make further demands on itself. (There is nothing monotonous or merely repetitive in this, since the diversity of things and events in the world is immense, and since renewal is also prescribed here as the law of the non–self-identical).

To make a thing of a subject—to render it unfulfilled and unfulfillable [*inaccomplissable*], to open it to the endless possibility of its affecting itself. Thus, to place the thing and place oneself with the thing, or rather, by the thing, in a disposition of pleasure—desiring and suffering in oneself an infinitude *outside the self* that offers the most rigorous truth of the self. Art truly does not stem from human subjectivity's attempts to figure or model a world in its guise, but rather, in art, the world reasserts itself prior to man, through man yet beyond him, so as to recreate itself.

This is nothing other than a "re-creation" of the world. That out of nothing comes form, or that nothing becomes form—in other words, distinction, separation, and opening. The *nothing*—the "thing" itself, *res, rem*—as reality of the displacement by which *that displaces itself* and *that distinguishes itself*. Distinction of the earth and sky, distinction of regions of space, of places and their times, of edges and limits, of the inanimate and the animate, of the conscious and the unconscious, of *self* and *that*—in a certain way, it is the same continuous-discontinuous distinction, absolutely archaic and always new, which goes from the nothing that a divine line divides to the line by which a drawing recovers from nothing the thickness of the received world, and thus further demands and desires the divine, in other words, the common divider of forms (alternatively, others might say: attributing the truth of his work to the divine). What we call art is nothing other than the ultimate and, for this reason, endlessly played out resurgence of division and distinction—that the gesture by which a world forms *itself* is distinguished in itself. That in addition this gesture might be thought of as a religious creation, or that it is questioned in a scientific mode ("the big bang," "string" theory . . .), or that it might be the object of metaphysical speculation—ultimately, all of that matters little in relation to the ways in which artistic gesture is thought in act, and in an endlessly renewed act.

Sketchbook 15

"The mechanism of the body makes its force [*puissance*] felt in the imagination. Gestures may draw, with an errant pencil, a form in front of the eyes that will fix these gestures in place and will open to daydreaming like a past and a history. The force of the imagination is defined by the mechanism of the body, which changes the action of things and at the same time makes use of them. The imagination consists of judging the presence, situation, and nature of objects according to the order of affections of the human body. The play of the imagination consists in the succession of corporeal states. No doubt judgment, emotion, gesture, and departure from the body together create vision."

—Alain, *System of the Fine Arts*

"The attitudes of the head and arms are infinite in number, and so I shall not undertake to give any rule for them, but simply say that they should be easy and agreeable with different inclinations, and the joints that are there should be united intelligently, so that they will not seem to be pieces of wood."

—Leonardo da Vinci, *Notebooks*

"[For Vasari] the notion of *disegno* would make it possible to justify artistic activity as 'liberal,' and no longer artisanal, because the word *disegno* was a word of the mind as much as a word of the hand. *Disegno*, then, *served to constitute art as a field of intellectual knowledge* . . . *Disegno* was effectively a magic word for him, first because it is polysemic, antithetical, infinitely manipulatable. It is almost a floating signifier—and Vasari did not hesitate to use it as such. . . . It is a descriptive word and it is a metaphysical word. It is applicable to the hand of man, but also to his imaginative *fantasia*, to his *intelleto*, and also to his *anima*—as well as, finally, to God the creator of all things. It comes from the vocabulary of the studio, where it designates the form obtained on a support by the charcoal or crayon of the artist; it also designates the sketch, the work in gestation, the project, the compositional schema, and the layout of the lines of force. It speaks the rule that presides over all of his technique, the *buona regola* of the painter, the one that gives rise to the *retta misura* of the line—in short, to the *disegno perfetto*."

—Georges Didi-Huberman, Confronting Images

"The deeper he looks, the more readily he can extend his view from the present to the past, the more deeply he is impressed by the one essential image of creation itself, as Genesis, rather than by the image of nature, the finished product.

—Paul Klee, On Modern Art

The Line's Desire

The line that divides and draws a form is similar to the arrow fired by a bow. The bow's tension is discharged in an instant, in a release of forces. But the relaxation of the bow manifests itself in the release [*jet*] of the arrow, as the relaxation of the sexual organ is expressed in orgasm [*le jaillir*], where the organ itself *rises up* [*s'enlève*], in all senses of the word.[45] The released arrow does not go toward any target; it only releases itself and its trajectory [*sa lancée*].[46] German says *Entwurf*, sketch [*jetée*], first draft [*premier jet*], *initial sketch* [première pensée], as historians of art say. The French say *esquisse* (which retains the idea of speed) and "*ébauche*" ("to give form to an unformed blur"). The English say *draught*, the drawn line that has not yet become a *drawing* but is drawn in the swiftness of its release.

The sketch not only retains the privilege of the endeavor, of the initial state whose pertinence would be genetic or genealogical. Its privilege is more essential, as every period of drawing has known. The sketch conveys the force of the release [*envoi*], that which the impetus reveals of a design deeper and more secretive than any form's aim [*visée*], a search or attempt that is only secondarily up for examination because it is first of all what sets the tone and opens the direction. The sketch does not disappear into the drawing; on the contrary, drawing exists only insofar as it retains the sketch within it, always released again, drawn, given impetus—in other words, insofar as it retains speed and releases it again, which is not a secondary property but the specific quality of *what goes straight to the target without there being a target*. This does not mean that the sketch necessarily succeeds, but rather that it makes known previously unknown stakes. What was only design becomes drawing for the first time—in other words, it leaves intention or aim in order to enter into the tension of the gesture alone and its abandon, its way of running a risk. The beginning thus equals the end, and makes an end in itself. Not the beginning in the sense of a stable point to which we can refer but endless, indefinable, infinite beginning, a beginning that will have always begun before beginning, in an antecedence that is impossible to situate (in a body, in a hand, in the head, in an emotion, etc.).

One could also say that we take leave of the project to give place to the draft [*jet*], or again, that we take leave of theory for practice. None of these expressions will be able to account for the incommensurable displacement of rupture and change, which is not a question of scale or register but of nature—where there was distance and stable positions (i.e., someone in front of sheet of paper, without always knowing whether there is a definite project, something other than the simple disposition of paper and pencils, now there is suddenly a mark [*tracé*], from the very first moment, a gesture's imprint [*trace*], and with it an irreducible desire of the line (to recall Matisse's expression).[47]

What is so noteworthy in this expression is that it does not play with metaphors. It does not claim that the line had a desire that in reality we know to be the desire only of the draftsman, a desire that would in itself be without any kind of impulse or intention. The tone of the phrase is not just playful. Matisse truly means to say that the line has desire that must be followed. It has desire because this desire is not what we call the artist's subjective disposition, any more than it is not (metaphorically or fantasmagorically) the inanimate being that is the traced line. The line is not an inert thing or a psychical projection. It is quite precisely a sketch, release, or casting out [*la jetée*], for which a hand (and with it all the body to which it is attached) and a line (the tiny deposit of lead or charcoal) come together thanks to each other (each responsible for the other)—an autonomous subject in terms of an impetus, escape or flight, tendency, vector, good fortune, grace, talent, gift or inspiration, or genius. One day it will be necessary to return to these discredited terms, not in order to restore their former credit but to revive again the question or aporia of what they are incapable of naming even though we cannot avoid designating it. Between the hand and the trace, in the pencil, quill, ballpoint pen, or charcoal crayon's impetus, in the movement that goes from the hand to the mark and flows back from the mark to bend the hand once again—in all this, an impulse is tapped, an energy is gathered from an entire culture and history, an entire thought or experience of the world comes to be gathered in the vibration of the mark [*trait*].

The *line* is not a poor resource for designating as its origin this point of contact between a thought and a gesture, between a sensibility and an activity, this indivisible and mobile point where a form and with it a manner are born—all the maneuverability and joint manipulations of what is *put into action* [mise en œuvre], in other words, bringing into appearance what is not hidden or given but invents itself in its gesture. For the line is the point itself—this non-point of birth, its self-origin stripped away [*dérobée*]—in the process of dividing space, dividing it by disposing and forming it, informing it by hollowing it out and affecting it, opening new possibilities for other spacings, in other words, for displacements and proximities, envelopments and avoidances, for folds, curves, departures, and returns. The *line* does nothing other than mobilize and draw forward a point of truth, and so it is in this way that it has—or rather it is—a desire. It is the point where it suddenly appears possible to go from nothing to something, to go from formless attachments and inherences to the form of detachments and distinctions. In fact, truth is only distinction. As Spinoza writes, it is in this way that truth manifests itself (*veritas seipsam patefacit*). Visual, sonorous, gestural, or tactile, delineation distinguishes, differentiates, distributes, and disposes at the same time as it disappears into its own movement.

This can all be "emotion"—there is indeed feeling and touch involved here. However, it is not simply the subject's affection in the psychological or "interiorizing" sense of the word. At bottom [*en son fond*], it is rather the setting in motion [*ébranlement*] of a machine, the most delicate of machines. It is the releasing of processes and circuits, transmissions and relays that detach and disseminate delineation *for pleasure*. This should be understood as the pleasure of delineating, in other words, for aspiring to the self alone, for the *repetition* in the original sense (demanding again) of what can only demand, call, or extend itself toward itself, toward a contour, figure, identity, or sense. The line's desire—or the line as desire—is thus a way of pleasing oneself to one's self, but to this lineal self always drawn in front of itself and always effaced in its origin, where the gesture will have preceded the tracing out [*tracé*], where an entire body will have preceded the gesture and an entire thrust (impulse, pressure) mobilized the body. An entire thrust—an entire thought, a weighing [*toute une poussée: toute un pensée, une pesée*].

Similarly, the *lineal self* is desire—not conscience, intention, or imagination, or even affect *in the strict sense*, but resounding noise [*retentissement*], the singular resonance of a point of truth. In light of what we have referred to as a "machine," it is possible to name this "an artist," or "a creator," or again, to say "his drawing," "his line," "his style," "his manner," or "his thought." All that counts is that the truth is implicated here in the way it should be—absolutely distinct, without ambivalence, and perhaps, in conclusion, without language as well (including poetry), without *signifiance*, creating signs differently, de-signating. But it is truth in itself, as such—that there is distinction, or idea, what is called "form," whose Latin name also implies beauty (*forma, formosa*).

And so, finally: What of the beautiful? That it is the splendor of the true, in other words, the sudden illumination [*éclat*] by which the truth appears. Not a ring of glory or brilliance attached to this appearance, for this splendor does not have a sparkling or sumptuous being, not unless one confounds profusion with satisfaction, because the beautiful cannot be filled, satisfied, or sated. Rather, it is the sudden illumination of the thing—the truth—that is in fact only its sudden illumination and the fact that it illuminates suddenly. It suddenly illuminates when a form rises up [*s'enlève*] distinctly—this is a body, this is its idea, this is its line and its most proper demarcation, its closure and its dis-enclosure conjoined together.

Beauty is the design of the true, its desire to burst open [*éclater*]. This desire detaches itself and becomes line—contour, melody, dance or phrase, story or recital, montage or palette, volume, grain, frame or cadence; it is always the desiring line and the desire to please itself in its own truth.

Because beauty is the sudden illumination of the true, it is also the truth's desirable character, and for this reason it communicates with the good, even if it is not to be confused with it. For the ancients, the true, good, and beautiful become transformed in one another. It was said that nothing is desirable that does not relate itself to itself according to its truth and that is not properly what it is or has to be. But if the "proper" is what there is given to be [*il y a à être*], then it is never given, never accomplished, never *made enough* or satisfied [*assez fait, satisfait*]. The proper and the propriety of the proper are not appropriable—it is not of being but "to being" (which can be transcribed in these terms: "to be" is not a state but a transitivity, the act of relating oneself toward the self [*s'envoyer vers soi*]). There is never any "enough" for any propriety, and its truth, which is its appearance, must always come back to showing itself as unachievable—an infinitely open transformation in all form by all beautiful form. Beauty is in the infinite relation. It exposes the infinite extension of a finite or finished form.

The unachievable here does not exist because of a defect. On the contrary, it provides the measure of *perfection*, which should be understood not as a completion but as in excess of all "making"—"perfect" becomes what exceeds "making," fabrication, production, or reproduction. Such a "making" is also inseparable from "undoing," just as for Blanchot all work finds its truth in unworking [*désœuvrement*]. But this undoing does not occur from a doing, fact, or what is "perfect," like a belated event or accident. The undoing is present at the beginning of making. It has already divided the beginning from itself, separating it from its "perfectionist" aims. The work (or artist or line) still desires perfection, but this is a perfection that retains within itself the (active and passive) force of an infinite availability.

This is why one must never ask oneself how ethics and aesthetics can be joined together, or why, on the contrary, they must be separated. If we retain the term, aesthetics is in itself an ethics in that it gives itself the supreme rule not to be satisfied with anything and to measure its pleasure by the desire not to be satisfied. The ruination of ethics is always in becoming fixated on a good instead of thinking with Plato of the Good as *beyond being* [au-delà de l'étant], or with Kant, who demands liberty as *the power to begin again*, and consequently whose Idea is Form beyond all form, or drawing whose line crosses all contour.

In quite different terms, beautiful form—that is, *drawing* not in the extensive sense of the term (i.e., all types of mark) but, on the contrary, in the profoundly comprehensive sense of what *draws itself*, distinguishes itself, extends itself—opens a revelation. Revelation is quite different from the appearance of something that was hidden. It is, rather, the appearance of what was never hidden, having never been given in any way, as when one says that a talent or artistic gift is revealed—for example, the young shepherd Giotto. One will never be able to trace this talent or gift back to any previous "form" [*germe*] or "potential" according to a causal or reproductive sequence of events. Revelation is neither given nor posed. On the contrary, it *reveals itself* as non-given, and it manifests itself in a newness irreducible to any prior condition. This is why there is a history of art, a history of the endless multiplicity of forms, which do not illuminate any form buried in the depth of things or any prior schema, not even and especially not a schema, idea, or concept of "art." On the contrary, what reveals itself and what *draws itself*—what announces itself, what gives itself to sense—in an incessantly renewed way is nothing other than this: that the world never conforms to a pre-given plan but its truth is inextricable from its drawing/design in perpetual formation and transformation.

In all its forms, in all its allures and ways—graphic, sonorous, dancing, or others—drawing designates this design without project, plan, or intention. Its pleasure opens onto this infinitude.

Sketchbook 16

"Drawing is the probity of art"

—Ingres

"Painting at Farnesia, Michelangelo gave Daniel endless advice. One day he even came to visit him and, not finding him, he climbed on the scaffolding and drew a huge head with charcoal. It is still there. Daniel respected it and did not put color on it so that posterity could know more about Michelangelo, even when he was playing."

—Stendhal, *The Italian Schools of Painting*

"A pleasure that the entire soul approves results from the beautiful."

—Joseph Joubert, *Thoughts*

"under the eyes again the
   figure [*figure*] is born from the line
that slices
this extraordinarily fleshy volume, as if
intact
           the instant
   where the painter himself is in front
of the real, and that instant where the real unbeknownst
to itself comes up to him—two distinct instants suddenly
confounded,
   and the figure on which in turn I
   was fixed takes body like fire to my own
eyes"

—André du Bouchet, *Notebook*

"We are enveloped by the morning's twilight—things are barely perceptible; the sun rises: the form of things is drawn; the sun climbs: things are illuminated and become more marked in all their plenitude. I do in my paintings what the sun does to nature."

—Gustave Courbet, cited by P. Courthion in
Courbet by Himself and His Friends

Notes

Translator's Note

1. *Le plaisir au dessin: Carte blanche à Jean-Luc Nancy* (Paris and Lyon: Hazan and Musée des Beaux-Arts de Lyon, 2007).

2. *Jean-Luc Nancy, Le plaisir au dessin* (Paris: Galilée, 2009).

3. See "Drawing Pleasure: A Conversation Between Alexander Düttmann and Jean-Luc Nancy," an exchange organized by Daniele Rugo for InC (Research Group In Continental Philosophy), which took place at Goldsmiths, University of London, in October 2007.

4. See Jean-Luc Nancy, "The Birth of Breasts, " tans. Kimball Lockhart, in *The Eight Technologies of Otherness*, ed. Sue Golding (New York: Routledge, 1997), 132–40; a translation of the full 2006 book publication by Éditions Galilée, *La naissance des seins, suivi de Péan pour Aphrodite* is forthcoming in Jean-Luc Nancy, *Corpus II: Writings on Sexuality*, trans. Anne O'Byrne (Fordham, 2013).

The Pleasure in Drawing

1. [The term *tracé* relates to the verb *tracer*, "to draw." It is translated here as "tracing out," although the term also evokes an outline, a layout, the plotting of a line, or ruling a line.—Trans.]

2. The expression "formation of forms" comes from Juan Manuel Garrido's remarkable book on Kant's "forms of sensibility." See Juan

Manuel Garrido, *La formation des formes* (Paris: Galilée, 2008). Prior to Garrido's specific elaboration of this term, "the formation of forms" had been used in a more thematic way by Jean-Christophe Bailly in his book on Piotr Kowalski, from whom he borrows the term. See Jean-Christophe Bailly, *Piotr Kowalski* (Paris: Hazan, 1988).

3. In general, there is neither metaphor nor comparison between artistic fields or registers—there is a general contagion. *Drawing* affects music in the same way as *timbre* affects the graphic arts. *Color, model, brilliance, note, touch, leap, figure,* and *rhythm* are some of the terms from which this contagion or general communication of the arts draws, essential in that this contagion also designates the constitutive impossibility of providing a single, unitary, and univocal determination of what "art" means. All these contagions and contacts respond to the multiple allures of a differential sensibility between aesthetic fields, a differential that responds to the differential constitutive of sensibility in general—to feel is also to distinguish. Sensation *distinguishes itself* in order to be itself, and the sensibility—or sensuality, it's all the same—specific to an aesthetic field proceeds from an intensified distinction, until it becomes the distinction that is an artist's own—a style, a gesture, an allure.

4. See Claire J. Farago, *Leonardo da Vinci's* Paragone: *A Critical Interpretation with a New Edition of the Text in the* Codex Urbinas (Leiden: E. J. Brill, 1992), 241.

5. [In translating *disponibilité* as "affordance," I am drawing on a term from contemporary design, one that suggests the way in which something is open to use.—Trans.]

6. Roger de Piles, *The art of painting, and the lives of the painters: containing, a compleat treatise of painting, designing, and the use of prints* . . . (London, 1706), 44.

7. In texts devoted to art, it is disconcerting to see how a French author is able to pass from one meaning of the word to the other, or from one word to the other in the same orthography. (Félibien offers us several examples.) Present-day Italian retains both meanings in the same word, *disegno*.

8. We have no intention here of returning to the history of words and concepts in which the specific problem of *disegno* and *drawing* has been played out since the Renaissance, or the role played by this problem in the formation of the modern concept of *art* and the complex

values to which it is attached. Nor is it a question of taking up the long history of disputes over the supremacy of drawing or color, the sketch and the achieved *tableau*, or, again, the existence or not of "lines" in nature. These various histories and debates have been addressed by numerous historians and well-known theorists, including (to cite only a few): in Georges Didi-Huberman, *Confronting Images: Questioning the Ends of a Certain History of Art*, trans. John Goodman (University Park, Pa.: Pennsylvania State University Press, 2009), taken up again by Daniel Payot in *Effigies: La notion d'art et les fins de la resemblance* (Paris: Galilee, 1997). For the relation with color, see Jacqueline Lichtenstein, *The Eloquence of Color: Rhetoric and Painting in the French Classical Age*, trans. Emily McVarish (Berkeley: University of California University Press, 1993), and Max Imdahl, *Farbe: Kunsttheoretische Reflexionen in Frankreich* (Munich: W. Fink, 1987). My proposal here concerns not knowledge but pleasure—it is pleasure that I would like to share, a pleasure that is invariably in excess of all knowledge that attempts to draw near it.

9. In this context, one might examine compulsive scribbling in the margins of books, in notebooks, or on scraps of paper. One should also consider the importance of speed and quick sketches in *tags* and *graffiti*, without forgetting, beyond drawing in the strict sense, humming, murmuring, or even sketches of rhythmic movements.

10. See Gilles Deleuze, "Desire and Pleasure," trans. Ames Hodges and Mike Taormina, in *Two Regimes of Madness: Texts and Interviews 1975–1995*, ed. David Lapoujade (Cambridge: MIT Press, 2007), 131 (trans. modified).

11. See Theodor W. Adorno, *Aesthetic Theory*, trans. Robert Hullot-Kenner (Minneapolis: University of Minnesota Press, 1997), 13 (trans. modified).

12. [Nancy refers often to a *trait*, which can be translated in several ways, including both "mark" and "line." As in English, *trait* stems from the Latin *trahere*, "to draw." What is lost in English translation is the sense in which *trait* is not only a line, graphic stoke (as in a "brushstroke"), or distinguishing mark (as in the artist's "touch") but also the process or action by which the line or mark is made, as in the drawing of a line across a surface, or the way a line is drawn (in the sense that a

curtain is drawn). At the same time, Nancy associates the *trait* with *retrait*, which (following Derrida) evokes in French the *trait* that is exposed to repetition, and so re-draws itself, as well as suggesting what withdraws or draws back. This in turn suggests an act of inscription that traces itself in withdrawing or drawing back the very incision in which an inscription takes place.—Trans.]

13. [The French here is "c'est de cet infini que la pensée, ici, a le dessein"—which can also be read as "thought aims for this infinity" or "thought designs this infinity."—Trans.]

14. Even when art associates pleasure with a manifest displeasure with regard to values, conventions [*convenances*], and forms that are already given. This is a question to which we will return in greater detail.

15. Can one say that this phrasing celebrates an auto-eroticism? That would be to misunderstand how Eros undoes and replays quite differently the relation between the "auto" and the "allo," just as it undoes and reopens differently the rhythmic beat of desire and pleasure—these two movements answer one another (desire of the other for pleasure of the same, desire of the same for pleasure of the other, pleasure of the desire of one by the other, desire of pleasure that renders the same other and thus more same than the same, etc.). In truth, Eros only enjoys desiring, through which it is at work in art without itself working. We will return to this question of the erotic in art.

16. See Heinrich Wölfflin, *Principles of Art History: The Problem of the Development of Style in Later Art*, trans. M. D. Hottinger (New York: Dover, 1950).

17. Félibien, *Entretiens sur les vies et sur les ouvrages des plus excellents peintres anciens et modernes* (Paris: Sebastien Mabre-Cramoisy, 1685), 3: 162.

18. [Nancy frequently plays with different senses of the verb *tendre*, which suggest at once extension, aim, and striving toward something.—Trans.]

19. [*Significance* is distinguished from *signification* and suggests an opening or gesture of sense rather than the signifying process, the movement toward a concept (the signified).—Trans.]

20. [Nancy is referring here to the concept of the "body without organs" in the writings of Gilles Deleuze and Félix Guattari.—Trans.]

21. [Nancy is referring to Wassily Kandinsky's *Point and Line to Plane*, trans. Howard Dearstyne and Hilla Rebay (New York: Dover, 1979).—Trans.]

22. The analysis that follows intersects in a number of ways with the much fuller analysis undertaken by Hubert Damisch in *The Judgment of Paris*, trans. John Goodman (Chicago: University of Chicago Press, 1996), regarding the origin or sexual nature of beauty and aesthetic pleasure. (Damisch holds to what Freud says about beauty rather than art.) At the same time, the analysis differs in principle: on the one hand, by drawing on Freud's distinction between two "pleasures," and on the other, by diverging from any schema of derivation or genesis between sex and the sense of the beautiful. To my mind, it is together and through the same Eros that sensuality and an aesthetic suddenly appear and divide themselves out—nothing comes first, only the infinity of desire. At the same time, moving in the direction of myth and what is archaic but not primitive, Damisch also diverges quite clearly from any derivative schema.

23. The texts in question here are Sigmund Freud, *Three Essays on the Theory of Sexuality*, vol. 7 of *The Standard Edition of the Complete Psychological Works of Sigmund Freud*, ed. and trans. James Strachey (London: The Hogarth Press and the Institute of Psycho-analysis, 1953), and *Jokes and Their Relation to the Unconscious*, vol. 8 of *The Standard Edition* (1960), two texts written by Freud at the same time that refer to one another.

24. However, Freud does sometimes distinguish this "diversion" from what we usually understand by "perversion," thereby opening, as it were, a broader legitimacy for the pleasure of form or forms.

25. Erotic pleasure, both the support and the *analogon* of aesthetic pleasure, as we will see, would be that which is not communicated—first of all, not from one to all, and not becoming a work, but not from one partner to another, either—for it is not about communication but about contagion. No doubt there is no communication without contagion, and vice versa; all the same, these are two distinct focal points of an ellipse of the *common*.

26. Jacques Lacan, *The Ethics of Psychoanalysis 1959–1960*, bk. 7 of *The Seminar of Jacques Lacan*, trans. Dennis Porter (New York: W. W. Norton & Co, 1992), 152.

27. When understood in the modern sense of "art," this expression contains at once a confused seduction (Eros in artistic practices) and an assured deception (we know that what we call "fornication" [*l' "œuvre de chair"*] is nothing within the order of the work).

28. In order to examine the idea of "sublimation" as presented by Freud—particularly because it remains ill-defined and ultimately unexplored by Freud himself—would be the work of another project. Nevertheless, it is interesting to note that Freud distinguishes two types of successful transformation of suppressed or restrained sexuality—on the one hand, it can produce a conversion of tension into active energy turned toward the world, as in the man of action, the zealot fighting for a cause, the reformer, or the savant, while on the other, there can be a renunciation, at least temporary, of libidinal satisfaction and a transfer to non-erotic goals. This second case is close to the artist's concerns (see Freud's "Types of Onset of Neurosis," 1912). This difference can also be seen in the difference between energy being put to use for more "elevated" ends by the abstinent subject and, by contrast, incitement given to a "stimulating" activity by the subject's own sexual activity. This is the case with art, and Freud can even write that "an abstinent artist is scarcely possible" (see his essay "'Civilized' Sexual Morality and Modern Nervous Illness," 1908). We should not forget that art here embraces all fields, from literature to music to visual arts. In other terms, knowledge and action divert the libido, whereas art extends and revives it. Or yet again, a converted libido is displayed in science, religion, and politics (in the terms mentioned above—a contagion entirely converted into communication), whereas art affirms a growing eroticism (a communicative contagion). No doubt this is not without consequence for reflections on art (here we might judiciously recall Nietzsche's phrase "without large quantities of sexual energy, there would be no Raphael!"), as well as for a very suggestive discrimination between "sublimation" through conversion to the non-sexual ("cultural" or "civilizational"), and another through the sexual irrigation of the "cultural." The second type does not lend itself as well as the first to the opposition between "fore-pleasure" and "terminal pleasure," or to the entirely "economic" idea of pleasure as entropy. To conclude, we should emphasize the following: what undermines an idea

114

like that of "sublimation" is the opposition that subtends it from top to bottom, echoing the motif of a progression from one to the other and from a primitive stage to an evolved stage. When one speaks of man, one must, on the contrary, always begin by rejecting these schemes of ascension and progression, since everything is given at once and right from the outset—sex and art, desire and culture, the modest and the sublime—all at once, one in the other, one by the other.

29. Other texts by Freud authorize this assimilation, provided one notes that he refuses to confuse what he calls "perversion" with that which he usually designates as an "anomaly," as he comes to phrase it. For Freud, the word *perversion* first of all characterizes a behavior that does not aim for a basic sexual finality where "discharge" triggers procreation.

30. Karl Marx, *Gundrisse: Foundations of the Critique of Political Economy*, trans. Martin Nicolaus (London: Penguin, 1973), 111.

31. [The phrase *à la dérobée* suggests "secretly" or "furtively," but can also suggest a stripping away or exposure.—Trans.]

32. More precisely, if not right at the body [*à même les corps*], Eros is incommunicable sensuality, and it remains so in art insofar as it is at issue there. Reciprocally, insofar as it is active in Eros, art inscribes there a communicable sensuality.

33. See Friedrich Hölderlin, *Essays and Letters on Theory*, trans. Thomas Pfau (Albany: State University of New York Press, 1988), 101. [In the original German, it is Hölderlin who introduces the French term *moyen* ["means"] in parenthesis.—Trans.]

34. I make this empirical remark (certain drawings are colored, others not) only to avoid the mistake of separating form and color. "Form" is determined little by little as line, mark, tracing out, and is extended to an impulse or thrust that is played out across all sensible registers. Though I will not address the question of color further, it is important to emphasize that even on an empirical level all drawing is colored (at least, color as from pencils). If drawing *opens* space, color *covers* this opening (this is its primary meaning). It is not that it closes it off, but rather that it keeps it secret.

35. ["Compearance" translates *comparution*, as suggested in Nancy's essay "La Comparution/The Compearance: From the Existence of

'Communism' to the Community of 'Existence,'" trans. Tracy B. Strong, *Political Theory* 20, no. 3 (1992): 371–98.—Trans.]

36. Allow me to refer here to my book, *L' "il y a" du rapport sexuel* (Paris: Galilée, 2001), forthcoming in English translation by Anne O'Byrne in Jean-Luc Nancy, *Corpus II: Writings on Sexuality*, trans. Anne O'Byrne (Fordham, 2013).

37. Leonardo da Vinci, *The Notebooks*, ed. Edward MacCurdy (London: Jonathan Cape, 1938), 1:106.

38. William Blake, "The Marriage of Heaven and Hell," in *The Poems of William Blake*, ed. W. H. Stevenson (New York: W. W. Norton & Co., 1972), 110.

39. It is not possible here to address the discussion concerning the definition and limits of pornography.

40. Giorgio Vasari, *Lives of the Most Eminent Painters, Sculptors, and Architects*, trans. Gaston du C. de Vere (London: Macmillan and Co. and the Medici Society, 1912–14), xlii.

41. Ibid, 72.

42. No doubt there exist any number of Stoic and Christian traditions, followed by Tristan, Hamlet and Romeo, Racine's Phaedra, etc.

43. See Jacques Derrida, "Desistance," in Philippe Lacoue-Labarthe, *Typography: Mimesis, Philosophy, Politics*, ed. Christopher Fynsk (Cambridge: Harvard University Press, 1989; rpt. Stanford, Calif.: Stanford University Press, 1998), 1–42.

44. [Drawing from the Latin *apparere*—"to appear, come in sight, make an appearance"—in which *parere* is "to come forth, be visible," I have translated Nancy's variations on *la paraître* or *l'apparaître* as "becoming visible."—Trans.]

45. [The verb *s'enlever* has the senses of both "to rise up" and "to remove," in the sense of taking something away from, as well as "to detach something from something else. "—Trans.]

46. [To continue *sur sa lancée* implies that something continues to forge ahead or continues in the same vein.—Trans.]

47. Here one should explicate the role of the album or sketchbook, drawing's handheld transcendental.